"Kyle Beshears has written, to my knowl[edge] [the first treatment] of sharing our Christian faith with our apatheistic neighbors: those who simply do not care about questions of God, life, the universe, and everything. Beshears understands the cultural influences driving religious uncocern, and he provides helpful and practical suggestions for engaging lovingly and productively with non-religious friends. If you want to understand and impact our post-Christian age, I highly recommend this excellent volume."

—**Tawa Anderson**, associate professor of philosophy, Oklahoma Baptist University

"We've been trained to share the gospel with adherents of other religions. We've been trained to share the gospel with people who viscerally oppose Christianity. But what about that vast middle of folks who . . . just don't care? As people live their lives unaware of their dire spiritual state, evangelism to the uninterested is perhaps our greatest challenge. *Apatheism* is the book you need to reach a world that doesn't seem to care. With painstaking scriptural focus and a heart full of compassion for the lost, Beshears lays out an approach that is both biblical and wise. If you care about the people who don't care, you need this book."

—**Daniel Darling**, senior vice president of communications, National Religious Broadcasters, and pastor of teaching and discipleship, Green Hill Church, Mt. Juliet, TN

"In a secular age, belief in God is not just contestable, but also uninteresting. There's a new virtue in town: apathy, especially when it comes to ultimate questions about God, meaning, and happiness. In *Apatheism*, Kyle Beshears expertly diagnoses the root causes of this indifference toward the God question and provides a helpful model for sharing the good news of Jesus to the uninterested. This book is essential reading for anyone seeking to effectively share the gospel with those who have lost touch with that deepest desire of every human heart for the pursuing love of God. "

—**Paul M. Gould**, associate professor of philosophy of religion and director of the MA in Philosophy of Religion program, Palm Beach Atlantic University

"A wise pastor once told me the biggest problem we face as Christian leaders is not hostility but apathy. And that's the problem that Kyle Beshears helps us address in this important new book. It's not helpful for us to answer questions few bother to ask anymore. Beshears helps us stoke the latent desires of unbelievers to *want* to want to believe."

—**Collin Hansen**, editorial director, The Gospel Coalition

"Twenty years ago, when I took my first steps into the field of apologetics, non-Christians sometimes misunderstood what I said and often despised the claims that I made—but no one ever said, 'I don't care whether these things are true or false.' But things have changed. Today, I hear some variation of this attitude over and over from high school and college students. It's not that these young people are vehemently anti-Christian; they simply don't care whether or not Christianity is true. Apologists in today's culture must have the capacity not only to respond to false claims about Christianity but also to engage with this growing sense of apathy toward faith. In *Apatheism: How We Share When They Don't Care,* Kyle Beshears provides a clear road map for sharing the gospel with those who claim that they aren't interested in whether or not the claims of Jesus are true."

—**Timothy Paul Jones**, vice president of doctoral
studies and chair of apologetics, ethics, and philosophy,
The Southern Baptist Theological Seminary

"In the New Testament, we often read about unbelievers being hostile toward Christians and their faith, but in many places today, we aren't dealing so much with a 'hostility toward the gospel' problem (though that's increasing in places), but with a 'happy without the gospel' problem. How do we reach *happy* pagans—those who are apathetic toward belief in God? With the rise in secularism in the West, including here in the States, I am thrilled to have Beshears's *Apatheism* in print. He provides us with important truth to consider in order to be both faithful and effective in our witness, as we radiate a contagious joy in Christ, and as we reflect the love of our God before a broken world in need."

—**Tony Merida**, dean and professor of preaching and theology,
Grimké Seminary; director of theological training, Acts 29; and
pastor for preaching and vision, Imago Dei Church, Raleigh, NC

"This book is for those who care to share with those who don't care. It's helpful for everyone to understand the religious, non-religious, and irreligious sentiments of our culture. Increasingly, vast numbers of people simply don't care about the question of God. You might remember the adage, 'You can lead a horse to water, but you cannot force it to drink.' But there are things we might do to make it want to drink, and that is in part what this book is about—how to get those apathetic to God to begin caring about the question of God and perhaps the gospel of Christ."

—**Corey Miller**, president and CEO, Ratio
Christi campus apologetics alliance

"'The harvest is abundant, but the workers are few. Therefore, pray to the Lord of the harvest to send out workers into His harvest,' says our Lord in Luke 10:2. That word for 'send' has often been explained to have a somewhat violent connotation, as if it must be done by force. Well, it has become clear to me that the Lord's method of answering this prayer in this age will mean waking and shaking potential harvesters from the sleep of apathy and preparing them for a harvest field where people are numbed by apathy. In *Apatheism*, Beshears helps us understand a prevailing mindset of the culture around us. This book helps us become better missionaries and better students of our culture, equipped to engage hearts and minds to see the need they don't know they have. This work is a gift!"

—**Noah Oldham**, senior director of deployment, Send
Network, North American Mission Board, and lead
pastor, August Gate Church, Belleville, IL

APATHEISM

How We Share

When They

Don't Care

APATHEISM

KYLE

BESHEARS

B&H

ACADEMIC

NASHVILLE, TENNESSEE

To my daughter, Whitney. May you be raised in a home where our affection for the Lord Jesus is evident in all that we do as a family.

CONTENTS

ACKNOWLEDGMENTS

How do we share the gospel when people don't care about God? This question isn't one that can be answered by just one person. Certainly, that's been the case for me. From discussions I've had with friends and colleagues to reading books and articles written by authors far sharper and wiser than me, I owe a lot to many. Thank you George Martin, Luke Bray, Nicholas Walburn, Stephen Lewis, Tim Stoner, Jared Halverson, Brad Hill, Dave Kakish, Brad Mills, Jud Daughtry, Tawa Anderson, Paul Gould, Chris Morgan, and my students for your engagement, support, feedback, and encouragement over the years. Thank you to the editors of the Evangelical Missiological Society Series and *Themelios* for allowing me a public space to discuss and debate my thoughts on this subject. Thank you to the team at B&H—Chris Thompson, Audrey Greeson, Sarah Landers, Jessi Wallace, and my anonymous reviewer—for your hard work and helpful suggestions. A special thanks to the church I pastor for giving me the opportunity to spend the necessary time to think, evangelize, and write. And a very special thanks to my beautiful bride, Heather, whose constant love and support sustained me. Finally, thank you, reader, for joining me on the Great Commission task of proclaiming the gospel to all people—even those who don't seem to care. *Soli Deo Gloria.*

PART 1 | APPROACHING APATHEISM

How can we share the gospel with someone who doesn't care about God? If you've ever tried it, you know it's tricky. You may have started by asking, "Do you believe in God?" But perhaps your neighbor responded as if you just asked for their opinion about the *Antiques Roadshow*. The question goes nowhere. Apathy swatted it down the way LeBron James would block a shot by Danny DeVito.

Most people who reply apathetically when God is mentioned aren't rude or hostile. In fact, they might have smiled and politely waited for the subject to change. It's not that they dislike God, and it's okay if you like him. But they just don't care. So the conversation turns toward something they do care about—something, *anything*, besides God. Because God means so much to you, this can be confusing. How can he not mean anything to other people?

When we think about common obstacles to evangelism, apathy doesn't typically come to mind. Instead, we imagine that the most difficult challenges come from religious beliefs, like Islam or Buddhism, and a-religious beliefs, like atheism and agnosticism. Most of the world's religions believe in some sort of god, but not the true and living God of Scripture. A-religious beliefs cast doubt over whether or not the divine even exists. Sure, it's difficult to bear witness to folks from these camps, but it's also fairly easy to strike up a conversation about God with them.

Imagine dialoguing with an atheist, a Muslim, and someone who doesn't care. The atheist asks the group why they think God could allow evil to exist in the world. Immediately, the Muslim offers a reply, and so do you. The atheist listens and states their opinion; then comes your response, and so on. A few minutes into the conversation, the group notices that one member is completely disengaged. She's been scrolling through social media on her smartphone the whole time. The atheist invites her into the conversation. "So, what do you think about God and evil?" he asks. She looks up from her phone, shrugs her shoulders, and returns to scrolling. She is bored out of her mind, having lost the reason and motivation to care about God long ago. By this point in her life, she might not even *want* to care.

This kind of apathy would have seemed very odd in the past. Long ago, nearly everyone cared about God, or, at the very least, some sort of supernatural being or beings. It would have been difficult to conceive of the world without some powerful deity, let alone feel indifferent toward it. For the longest time, God played an integral part in the lives of ordinary people. He created and sustained the cosmos. He commanded angels and foiled demons. He appointed monarchs and religious leaders to rule over earthly kingdoms and churches. He knit infants in their mothers' wombs and gave them every breath, from birth to death. He watched our lives, remembering our good and evil deeds for a final day of judgment. In the end, people would either spend eternity basking in the glory of his presence or wailing in the punishment of his wrath. Our lives—every aspect of them—revolved around God.

This was also true in nations that were not Christian. Throughout time and all over the world, whether people worshiped Allah, Vishnu, Zeus, or Ra, humanity has held a universal conviction that something beyond natural reality exists; in it we live and move and have our being (Acts 17:28). Regardless of what you believed, at least you were a believer.

The apostle Paul knew this well. During one of his missionary journeys, he preached in Athens, a cultural hub for the Roman Empire (Acts 17:16–21). Because of its rich history, the city attracted the region's best and brightest students, artists, and thinkers, all searching in their own way for a life of fullness, that is, the joyful life in which one is fully satisfied and flourishing in body, mind, and soul. Paul's preaching caught people's attention. They found his message intriguing, so they invited the "preacher of foreign deities," as they called him, to the Areopagus, a rocky outcrop used as a public forum to discuss and debate ideas (vv. 18–19).

To get there, Paul walked past elaborate monuments dedicated to the gods and their myths. One statue, in particular, caught his attention—a statue to the "unknown god" (Acts 17:23). The Athenians were apparently concerned that all the gods be included in their worship. But with so many deities in their mythology, who could keep track? To ensure they didn't inadvertently offend a forgotten god, the Athenians dedicated a statue to an "unknown god."[1]

Despite the vast gap between Christian and polytheistic beliefs, Paul knew that both he and the Athenians agreed on one thing—*theism*, or belief in a god. Paul shrewdly leveraged this shared conviction to make a case

---

[1] The precise meaning of the altar to the unknown god is, like the idol itself, not known. Ancient sources attest that Athens was furnished with altars to gods who were unknown. Charles H. Talbert, *Reading Acts* (Macon, GA: Smyth & Helwys, 2005), 153. F. F. Bruce suggested the statue Paul saw may have fallen derelict and, after restoration, the original inscription could not be recovered. Thus, the Athenians simply acknowledged the god's identity as lost to time. F. F. Bruce, *The Acts of the Apostles*, 3rd ed. (Grand Rapids: Eerdmans, 1990), 381. Paul, though, found more significance in their ignorance of this god. As Jaroslav Pelikan noted, the apostle seems to have pointed to a "presumably faceless and nameless and mythless" deity that he wished to make known. Jaroslav Pelikan, *Acts: Brazos Theological Commentary on the Bible* (Grand Rapids: Brazos Press, 2005), 194. Likewise, J. B. Lightfoot argued that Paul appealed to the anonymous idol "as evidence of an element of uncertainty in their religious confusion, in what they confessed, and he offered to reveal this to them." J. B. Lightfoot, *The Acts of the Apostles: A Newly Discovered Commentary*, vol. 1, ed. Ben Witherington III and Todd D. Still (Downers Grove, IL: InterVarsity Press, 2014), 232. James Dunn agreed, noting how in Paul's sermon he "proclaims no new god, but one they themselves recognized, albeit inadequately." James D. G. Dunn, *The Acts of the Apostles* (Grand Rapids: Eerdmans, 1996), 234–35.

for the gospel. He proclaimed with clarity the God whom the Athenians worshiped in ignorance (Acts 17:22–34). They yearned for something more than their philosophies and myths could offer, so much so that they had even dedicated a statue to this known-but-unknown god. Paul argued that the "unknown god" to the Greeks was known to the Christians, and he is the only true and living God (v. 23).

The apostle's speech is brilliant, inspired by the Holy Spirit; unsurprisingly, it's often cited by believers today as one of the best models for evangelism, especially as it relates to apologetics (i.e., defending the faith). Like Paul, we ought to take notice of the "gods" in whom our neighbors believe (or disbelieve). We lift the Lord Jesus high above these so-called "gods" because in him alone do people come to truth and eternal life.

In other words, contemporary evangelism based on the Areopagus model begins with a shared interest in the big questions about God and life. But what if the Athenians had been like your neighbor who didn't care about God? They wouldn't have found Paul's preaching intriguing but uninteresting, perhaps even unwelcome. And there would likely have been no statue to the "unknown god." If the statue were there, it would have been hidden behind creeping vines and layers of soot, evidence that the gods no longer captured the kind of interest they used to. How could Paul have argued that the "unknown god" is the true and living God if his audience couldn't care less about deity?

What if we live in an Athens without a statue to the unknown god?

The New Challenge of Apatheism

What made Paul's sermon so brilliant isn't merely *what* he said but *how* he said it. He delivered the timeless message of the gospel in a timely way, and his audience heard him. Every generation of Christians is tasked with doing the same thing: to understand their culture well so that they may bear witness to the gospel well. We are not the power that saves people. It is the redemptive work of the Holy Spirit that invades and renews hearts. But, by sheer wonder, God has invited us into this amazing task as ambassadors of his kingdom. Believers are redeemed by grace alone through faith alone in the person and work of Jesus Christ alone (Eph 2:8–9; Gal 2:16). Then those who are redeemed go into the world to proclaim the same gospel that saved them (Matt 28:18–20; Rom 10:17). In other words, God saves people through saved people, heralds who proclaim the good news of his kingdom. But deafening agents work to stop the ears of those whom God would call to himself. Scripture is filled with stories of how sin and disbelief deafen people to the voice of God, those who "are deaf, yet have ears" (Isa 43:8).

Our culture has a new kind of deafening agent caused not by disbelief but indifferent belief. This new agent is a complete apathy toward theism, or *apatheism*. This new *ism* has a different quality to it than other beliefs that seem related. Atheism believes that God does not exist; agnosticism believes that we can't know whether or not God exists; apatheism believes God's existence to be irrelevant. It says we shouldn't care about him at all.

Like most beliefs, apatheism doesn't stay in the mind. It seeps into our hearts, causing us to feel apathy toward God in our souls. Apatheism, then, is when a person *believes* God is irrelevant and *feels* apathetic toward him. It's both belief and feeling, thought and emotion, affecting the mind and heart.

This dispassion toward God is found most often in a society that is secular, comfortable, and distracted. I use the word *secularism* as philosopher Charles Taylor defined it. In his *A Secular Age*, Taylor argued that secularism isn't merely the absence of religious belief; rather, secularism occurs wherever belief in God seems difficult to hold and is merely one choice of belief among other options, thus rendering belief disputable.[2]

Comfort is a sense of existential safety and tranquility, the hollow peace and ease that come with living in a safe and prosperous society.

Distraction is the many ways our digital age offers relief from thinking about things beyond the moment. As Alan Noble put it in his *Disruptive*

---

[2] Charles Taylor, *A Secular Age* (Cambridge, MA: Harvard University Press, 2007), 1–3, 19. For an excellent introduction to Taylor's massive tome, see James K. A. Smith, *How (Not) to be Secular: Reading Charles Taylor* (Grand Rapids: Eerdmans, 2014).

Witness, the "constant distraction of our culture shields us from the kind of deep, honest reflection needed to ask why we exist and what is true."[3]

Each of these factors is like a strong wind that has blown our culture off course and shipwrecked us on an archipelago made up of islands of apathy where many lack the reason and motivation to care about God. As a result, many people may not even want to care about God because alternative explanations to our biggest questions have eclipsed belief in him, and religion (Christianity in particular) is not seen as offering a compelling avenue to satisfy humanity's deepest yearning for joy.

In this book, I want to consider ways that we can share the gospel with our apathetic neighbors. I will draw on personal experience and biblical concepts of happiness and joy to build a model of evangelism. This model will require us first to reflect on our own souls, determining whether or not we too have been affected by apathy. If so, we must recapture the joy of our salvation before we can explain and demonstrate to an apatheist that true and lasting joy is only discovered in a life spent in Christ and pursuing him. Then we can approach apatheism, dialoguing about the power and permanence of biblical joy, and how God alone offers us what our hearts long for the most.

Evangelism in an Apathetic Areopagus

I remember the first time I encountered apatheism. Years ago, my wife and I lived in England. My job relocated near Cambridge, allowing us the opportunity to live there. Cambridge is one of those cities where you don't need to do anything but meander to enjoy it. It's a stunning town and, even after a few years of living there, we found that meandering never got old.

One Saturday afternoon, I decided to visit my favorite bookstore, which sat just off the market square. It was a cold and dreary day, but I was determined to go. As I approached the market, I noticed a man standing

---

[3] Alan Noble, *Disruptive Witness: Speaking Truth in a Distracted Age* (Downers Grove, IL: InterVarsity Press, 2018), 3.

behind a long table; he was passing out flyers. I almost expected him to be there—he had consistently set up a booth in the market for months. The man, a Muslim, was trying to proselytize, and I do mean *trying*. I watched week after week as the pamphlets he managed to give away ended up in the nearby trash bin. I rarely saw him speaking with anyone.

That day, under the gloomy weather, he looked particularly dejected. Something in me empathized, so I bought two cups of coffee and approached him.

"Hey," I greeted him, extending one cup toward him.

He looked up from his table, first to the cup and then to me. "Hi," he replied with a bit of caution in his voice. "That's for me?"

I nodded. He took the cup, lifted the cover to inspect its contents, looked me in the eyes, and took a sip.

"Thanks, mate," he said.

We stood for a moment, sipping our coffee and surveying the busy scene. Dozens of people passed by the booth under the cover of their umbrellas, with shopping bags in hand. A few students whizzed by on bikes. No one stopped.

"Why the coffee?" he inquired.

"You just looked like you could use one today," I answered. "And, to be honest, I think this is something that Jesus would do." (Yes, that's right—I slipped in the Jesus angle up front.)

"Ah," he said, "so you're a Christian?" His tenor was genuine, like he had found an ally.

"Yes, I am. I belong to a church just around the corner from here."

"Well, then," he said, interrupting his sentence with another sip, "you know my pain all too well."

His reply took me off guard. How could I, a Christian, know his pain as a Muslim attempting to convert people to Islam? Surely he misspoke.

"I'm not sure that I know what you mean," I confessed.

He took a deep breath that ended in a sigh as he stared at the bustling market.

"These people," he said, pausing for a few moments. "They care nothing about God. How can that be?"

That's when it hit me. The fruitlessness of so many spiritual conversations I'd had there finally made sense. It wasn't that people were hostile to the gospel, which is what I had assumed. It wasn't even that they were too busy to be bothered with conversations about Jesus.

They simply didn't care.

After a long pause, the Muslim man broke the silence. "You and I may not agree on who God is, but at least we agree that he's important."

He was right. We didn't agree on the nature of God, but we shared the conviction that theism is essential. A few minutes later, we proved his point unwittingly. We talked about evidence in philosophy for God's existence, and we marveled at how the Creator left his fingerprints all over creation. But we disagreed, too. We debated the effects of sin on the human condition. We sparred over the role of Christ as our prophet-mediator, the meaning of the cross, and the historicity of his resurrection.

At that point in our conversation, a young man appeared from the crowd and approached us. He seemed interested in the spread of literature because his eyes scanned around the table.

The Muslim man beamed with hope.

"Oi, mate, how are you today?" he asked.

"Yeah, good," the young man replied.

"We were just talking about religion. Care to join?"

The young man declined. "Just looking for the trash bin, is all."

The Muslim motioned to its location as he tried to capture the man's attention.

"Are you sure? We're having a fascinating conversation about God."

"No," the young man reiterated. "The idea of God is just not that interesting to me, really." With a parting "cheers," he threw away some trash and headed back to the market. We both watched as he disappeared into the crowd.

"See?" asked the Muslim man.

"I do."

After we finished talking, I was no longer in the mood to hunt for books. As I walked home, the Muslim man's words echoed in my mind: "They care nothing about God. How can that be?"

He was right, and I had just seen it. How can it be that people care nothing about God?

I want to answer the Muslim man's question, but I want to do more than that. I want to explore ways that we can follow Paul's example of delivering the timeless message of the gospel in a timely way. We are on commission by our King to proclaim his good news everywhere, even in our age of apathy. Our task is to pierce through our neighbors' indifference to awaken their souls to the most abundant source of eternal joy. It won't be easy work, but the joy that comes from the harvest of this labor makes any other pale in comparison. What else could we ask for but to join in heaven's chorus of praise when figurative coins and sheep are found and when prodigal sons and daughters find their way home? This is the kind of joy that is expressed straight from the very source of joy itself, our God.

We'll begin by considering the factors and conditions that make something like apatheism possible. Once we understand how apatheism could arise in a culture, we can then explore it in detail. Lastly, and most importantly, we will consider how we might approach it with the gospel.

Chapter 1 | Cultural Conditions of Apatheism

Let's return to Cambridge for a moment. That market is old. Very old. It's been around since the Middle Ages. To put that into perspective, Islam was still a relatively new religion when people first began haggling over prices there.

Imagine transporting back in time to medieval Cambridge. You'd find yourself in a very different world. Not just in the obvious sense of looks and fashion and technology, but a whole different way of viewing everything.

Philosopher Charles Taylor argued this very point. He noted how people in medieval Europe lived in an enchanted world. They believed in God, who was separate and transcendent above his creation but also mysteriously immanent to it, very near and active. The universe was filled with natural and supernatural beings who shared spaces—farmers and spirits, blacksmiths and devils, kings and angels. The boundary between the natural and spiritual realms was thin, and it was often crossed; thus, everyone felt vulnerable to spiritual powers, whether good or evil.

If you were pierced by Cupid's arrow, you might actually fall in love with someone you didn't like. Demonic possessions and witches' curses were real threats, but God's Spirit kept evil at bay by indwelling the faithful and inhabiting sacred spaces and relics. People relied on God to bring rain and stave off drought, to appoint rulers, and to keep them safe from foreign invaders. They attended mass regularly, prayed daily, resisted the seven deadly sins, and contemplated their mortal standing before the Great Judge.

Medieval Europeans took God for granted, feeling his influence every day. They relied on him for their every need. For them, belief in God was the default position and disbelief in him was unthinkable. As the reformer John Calvin (1509–64) observed about his world, "No one will want to be considered as being entirely indifferent to personal religion and the knowledge of God."[1]

Fast-forward five centuries and Calvin's observation no longer holds true for everyone. Belief in God isn't default; it's optional. And, for many people, it's such a difficult and seemingly unnecessary belief to hold that they simply dismiss God altogether.

How did we go from being a world where people viewed God as critical to one in which he can seem so unimportant? In other words, for our purposes, where did apatheism come from, and why are people apatheistic?

Apatheism flourishes in a society where belief in God is contestable and diverse and the people are comfortable and distracted (see fig. 1.1). It's found wherever people pursue fulfillment without God because he's considered irrelevant to answering questions related to our origin, meaning, and joy.

Western society fits this description well. It's not guaranteed that your neighbor believes in God, or any god. For some people, it's not that they disbelieve because they've been convinced otherwise. They don't believe because they don't see the point. Affluent society tends to all our wants and needs, entertaining and amusing us. We live comfortably and distracted, which keeps us from contemplating the biggest questions of life.

To understand how apatheism is possible, we'll need to break this thought down piece by piece. First, we'll consider how our belief in God is both contested and varied because of secularism. Charles Taylor will help us see how secularism isn't merely skepticism or contestability of belief in God. Secularism is also pluralism, that is, the coexistence of multiple beliefs. For a culture to be secular means belief in God is *both* contestable and diverse.

---

[1] John Calvin, *Truth for All Time: A Brief Outline of the Christian Faith*, trans. Stuart Olyott (Edinburgh: Banner of Truth Trust, 1998), 3.

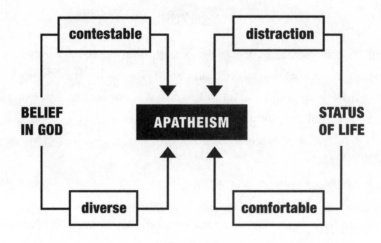

Figure 1.1

Four conditions contribute to the appearance of apatheism.
Belief in God is contestable and diverse, and our
status of life is comfortable and distracted.

Then we'll consider how the affluence of the American economy and modern technology keep us so comfortable and distracted that even thinking about God seems unnecessary. Alan Noble will help us see how technology has made it very difficult for us to consider the most important questions in life. In many ways, what follows springboards off Noble's thought in his *Disruptive Witness*, a book that I cannot recommend highly enough.[2] He also built on the work of Taylor to diagnose shortcomings in our witness caused by secularism and technology, and prescribed ways for us to rise above the current of our distracted age for the sake of the gospel. Noble persuasively demonstrated how secularism and technology have distracted us from God. Now, I want to argue in addition that secularism and technology, along with affluence, have also made us apathetic toward him.

---

[2] Alan Noble, *Disruptive Witness* (see part 1 intro., n. 3).

Secularism

In his massive tome *A Secular Age*, Charles Taylor asked a very similar question to the one we've asked. Namely, "Why was it virtually impossible not to believe in God in, say, 1500 in our Western society, while in 2000 many of us find this not only easy, but even inescapable?"[3] His answer, as the title of his book suggests, is secularism, but not in the way we might initially think.

We typically associate secularism with skepticism, that the idea of God is arguable and disputed. Secularism is synonymous with a-religious beliefs. It's an emphasis on the temporal rather than eternal; it means not pertaining to religion. And we assume that skepticism leads to indifference about God. This is true sometimes, but it's not always the case.

In fact, ironically, sometimes the opposite is true. Think about the hostility of the New Atheists, like Richard Dawkins and Sam Harris.[4] In his most recent popular-level book, *Outgrowing God*, Dawkins talks about God and religion quite a bit. He assures his readers that there's no need to believe in the former or practice the latter because science has propelled us beyond them both. In fact, he feels it's a sign of maturity if you don't believe, even though it might be difficult to let go. He ends his book imploring his readers to "take our courage in both hands, grow up and give up on all gods."[5] Elsewhere, Harris gave us a fundamental reason why: belief in God elicits "ignorance and fanaticism," which, in turn,

---

[3] Taylor, *Secular Age*, 25 see part 1 intro., n. 2).

[4] Selected works include Richard Dawkins, *A Devils' Chaplain* (Boston: Houghton Mifflin, 2004); *The God Delusion* (Boston: Houghton Mifflin, 2006); *Outgrowing God: A Beginner's Guide* (New York: Random House, 2019); Sam Harris, *The End of Faith: Religion, Terror, and the Future of Reason* (New York: W. W. Norton, 2004); *Letter to a Christian Nation* (New York: Random House, 2006); *Waking Up: A Guide to Spirituality without Religion* (New York: Simon & Schuster, 2014).

[5] Dawkins, *Outgrowing God*, 278.

oppresses people into fear.[6] So, belief in God ought to be dismissed. New Atheism, it turns out, cares quite a bit about God. It just cares about him in the opposite direction from believers. After all, authors like Dawkins and Harris have made a great deal of money debating theism and ridiculing religion. If every skeptic were apathetic toward the idea of God, who would buy their books?

Skepticism doesn't represent the totality of secularism. Instead, imagine secularism as a state in which it's okay either to disbelieve in God or believe differently than your neighbor, whether that belief has to do with God, gods, or nothing at all.[7]

It wasn't always like this, of course; as Taylor explained, a change in the way we think occurred some five hundred years ago. After that, Western society shifted from the position where "belief in God is unchallenged and indeed, unproblematic, to one in which it is understood to be one option among others, and frequently not the easiest to embrace."[8] Once, orthodoxy was default, although there were certainly some in the margins who believed differently. Now, in our secular age, orthodoxy itself is marginalized. Society allows for both unbelievers and believers, and all different kinds of believers at that.

For the purpose of our question, then, secularism leads to apatheism for two reasons: (1) secularism offers us an alternative explanation for the origin of the universe and meaning of life without appealing to the supernatural, thus permitting some people to lack a reason to care about God; and (2) secularism provides the fertile ground for pluralism (diversity of beliefs), thus robbing some people of a reason to care about God in a crowded field of competing "truths."

In both instances, skepticism and pluralism, a person can lose any reason to care about God, either because he's not needed to answer life's biggest

---

[6] Harris, *Waking Up*, 359.
[7] Taylor, *Secular Age*, 3.
[8] Taylor, 3.

questions or there are just too many answers to those questions, so it's better to relax and let the religious thinkers and philosophers sort out that mess.

Secularism as Skepticism

Let's consider the first reason, that belief in God is contestable. This is easy to understand because we're very familiar with the story of how secularism supposedly liberated us from the tyranny of ignorance and myths. It goes something like this: A few hundred years ago, we were blinded by religion. It hindered our ability to think, live, and organize society according to our conscience and reason. Our rational minds were imprisoned by superstition, and our lives were shackled to myth. Society submitted to the authority of some deity in the heavens and his representatives on earth.

We were trapped, like a damsel in distress, locked away in the castle of ignorance. But something changed. A knight named Enlightenment stormed the keep to rescue us. Science taught us that the supernatural isn't real (naturalism) because physical matter is the only thing that exists (materialism). Rationalism taught us how to organize our lives and society without appealing to some transcendent authority.

The Enlightenment brought a time of "withouts": the universe *without* God, philosophy *without* God, government *without* God. Science and reason cast an unflattering light on enchanted beliefs. Before, the existence of God was unquestionable. Afterward, belief seemed silly and childish. The world matured as it was *dis*enchanted. We stopped believing in God and devils once we started believing in science and reason. For some people, like Denis Diderot (1713–84), God became irrelevant altogether. As perhaps one of the first Enlightenment philosophers to exhibit apatheism, Diderot quipped, "It is very important not to mistake hemlock for parsley, but to believe or not believe in God is not important at all."[9]

---

[9] Denis Diderot, "Letter from Diderot to Voltaire, June 11, 1749," ed. Arthur M. Wilson, *Revie d'Historie Littéraire de la France* 51 (September 1951):

Nevertheless, some people still cared and believed. There was a dis-connect between Enlightenment thinkers in ivory towers and the common folk on farms. Unlike the elites, the peasants still believed, haunted by a sense that there was something more beyond the natural order of things.

That is, until ideas like Darwinism developed and saturated the public imagination, and, as philosopher Daniel Dennett argued, acting like a "uni-versal acid," ate through every traditional concept until only a "revolution-ized world-view" remained.[10]

So, we're told, the secularization of Western society is a story about subtraction. Once we removed God from the equation, we were left with human reason and desires to guide us into a new era of modernity. Armed with the power of criticism, we've come to understand that religion was merely an evolutionary tool that lost its value in the face of reason. Religion was the "sigh of the oppressed creature [and] opium of the people," accord-ing to Karl Marx, but rationalism liberated and sobered us to see religion for what it truly is—the illusion of an imaginary world.[11] The open-minded rely on empirical evidence, not superstition, to form beliefs, and have therefore freed themselves to "think, act, and fashion [their] own reality," claimed Marx.[12]

Today, for many people, God has become irrelevant because science and skepticism did away with needing him to explain the hows and whys of life. So God is irrelevant to how we imagine fullness. We know where we came from—a universal common ancestor from long ago. And we know our purpose. The narrative of Darwinism has set us on a trajectory of evolution and advancement.

258–60, quoted in Michael Buckley, *At the Origins of Modern Atheism* (New Haven, CT: Yale University Press, 1987), 225.

[10] Daniel C. Dennett, *Darwin's Dangerous Idea: Evolution and the Meanings of Life* (New York: Penguin, 1996), 63.

[11] Karl Marx, *Karl Marx: Selected Writings*, 2nd ed., ed. David McLellan (Oxford: Oxford University Press, 2000), 72.

[12] Marx, 72.

The meaning of life, then, isn't found in some religion or god; it's found in *us*. We ought to strive toward advancing and improving the human condition, to find our own fulfillment. That's where we find our joy, through altruistic living. We're only here for a short while. One day, we'll become nothing but dust as our consciousness ends and everything goes black forever. In the meantime, it's best to make the most of every moment by bringing goodness to the world, however you want to define "goodness."

Besides, religion can be a very contentious issue, so why should we let ourselves get worked up over imaginary superstition? This was the argument made by journalist Jonathan Rauch, who popularized the concept of apatheism in his *Atlantic Monthly* article, "Let it Be."[13] In the wake of the terrorist attacks of 9/11, Rauch denounced ideological fundamentalisms, whether religious (e.g., Salafi jihadism) or a-religious (e.g., Stalinism), as harmful to the progression and safety of a society. The solution, he claimed, was apatheism, which has a calming effect on all belief, regardless of its content. An ideologically dispassionate society is one undisturbed by radicalization.[14] Rauch's prescription may now be reality. Sociologist Steve Bruce observed that in a secular society religion is generally seen as a positive force that teaches morals and offers comfort to believers, but fervent belief, especially in public spaces, is frowned upon.[15]

In sum, if secularism means that belief in God is contestable, then some apatheists lack the reason to care about God because ideas like naturalism and materialism explain him away. So why care at all?

---

[13] Jonathan Rauch, "Let It Be," *Atlantic Monthly*, May 2003, 34–35. Rauch is commonly attributed with coining the term *apatheism*, a claim he did not make. The term was perhaps first used by Canadian sociologist Stuart Johnson to describe the kind of indifference toward religion evidenced in an ever-secularizing society. "The Correctional Chaplaincy: Sociological Perspectives in a Time of Rapid Change," *Canadian Journal of Criminology and Justice* 14 (1972): 179.

[14] Rauch, "Let It Be," 34–35.

[15] Steve Bruce, "Secularization and Its Consequences," *The Oxford Handbook of Secularism*, ed. Phil Zuckerman and John R. Shook (New York: Oxford University Press, 2017): 55–70, 67.

Secularism as Diversity of Belief

But, as Taylor pointed out, there's another way to look at secularism, which helps to explain a second reason why it gives rise to apatheism. Taylor argued that secularism isn't necessarily a story of subtraction but addition, which is why we have *more*, not *fewer*, beliefs after the Enlightenment.

Secularism doesn't simply mean that belief in God is contestable, which it is. Secularism also means that belief in God is diverse, that there are many different forms and alternatives to Christianity.[16] In other words, the West has abandoned the assumptions that God exists *and* that he exists exclusively in Christian terms.

Five centuries ago in the West, the existence of God was automatically assumed. It was nearly impossible not to believe in God, especially the tri-une God of Christianity. But today, belief in him is challenged by count-less alternatives. Consider how many beliefs live next to each other in the West: Roman Catholicism, Protestantism, atheism, agnosticism, Buddhism, Islam, and so on.

As Taylor put it, we have morphed from a society in which it was "vir-tually impossible not to believe in God, to one in which faith, even for the staunchest believer, is one human possibility among others."[17] So, if secular-ism was truly the acid that eroded religious belief, then why are so many religions still around? Moreover, why are there so many *new* religious move-ments like New Age and Scientology?

We tend to use "secular" as a synonym for "disbelief." To be "secular" means to reject religion. But, as Taylor argued, disbelief is only *part* of secu-larism, not the whole, because atheism, like theism, is one optional belief among many.[18] Atheism and Christianity coexist among a host of other options. True, in the aftermath of the Enlightenment, God seems less likely

---

[16] Taylor, *Secular Age*, 3.

[17] Taylor, 3.

[18] Taylor, 2–3.

to exist now than he ever did before, but skepticism is not the reigning champion. Belief hasn't eroded; it has fractured.

Taylor identified a shift in the way we think as the root cause of this fracturing. The shift was a relocation in where we find value, importance, and significance, or what he called "meaning."[19] "[In] the enchanted world," Taylor said, "meanings are not in the mind."[20] People believed things themselves *held* meaning. Religious relics and witches' cauldrons really did hold power in themselves, and both were caught up in a supernatural war between good and evil. And that's just the way it was.

But then the shift occurred to a "mind-centered view" where meaning was *assigned*, not *inherent, to* things. Meaning relocated from the external, objective world to our internal, mental wills. After the shift occurred, "things only have the meaning they do in that they awaken a certain response in us," e.g., feelings, desires, etc.[21] But no extranatural agent can change us.

Practically, this meant that witches and relics were no longer powerful by themselves. A person had to believe they held power. The thin line between the natural and supernatural thickened. We became *invulnerable* to the outside world as we isolated ourselves in our minds.

Granted, we were still affected by the world to some degree. Observations and interactions could change our minds and moods. But meaning still lies within us. We change our thoughts only if we *want* to, and our emotions change only when our brains secrete chemicals. Cupid's arrow and a witch's spells are powerless. No one actually believes that demon possession or voodoo dolls can affect us. We are closed systems, buffered from the outside world.

That's the significance of the shift. We sheltered ourselves from the external world, as Taylor explained, and as "buffered" selves, each of us

---

[19] Taylor, 31.
[20] Taylor, 32.
[21] Taylor, 31.

became masters of meaning.[22] Now, I am a rational, material thing whose "ultimate purposes are those which arise within me."[23] My mind is protected behind a firewall programmed to block any idea and experience I don't like and to permit any that I do. Meaning is what I make of it, and that's just the way it is.

Had I lived in the medieval world, I would have taken God and supernatural powers for granted. He would have been extremely important to me. But living in the modern world, I take materialism and my internal meaning making powers for granted. The center of all my thoughts, beliefs, and feelings is my mind, and it is possible to protect my mind from external influences. The most important source of meaning is me.

This buffering has had a profound impact on belief in God. As a buffered self, I am not meaningful because God has given *me* meaning. The opposite is now true. God is meaningful because I give *him* meaning. And if individuals are the ones creating meaning, then there are potentially as many beliefs as there are people. This is why secularism is not merely a-religious skepticism but also religious diversity.

The challenge to belief, then, isn't necessarily that it's under assault by skepticism (although it certainly is). Rather, there are too many beliefs to choose from, both religious and a-religious.

Imagine returning to the streets of medieval Cambridge. If you wanted to explore belief in God, where would you go? The local Roman Catholic parish. You had no other options. To reject Roman authority was to be branded a heretic, which resulted in exile or execution.

Now, fast-forward through the centuries to watch your options grow. During the Reformation, people began to rediscover the faith and reimagine Christianity. For them, the Catholic Church looked less like the gateway between heaven and earth and more like an obstacle for the biblical, rational Christian to overcome. These folks wanted to live the Christian faith,

---

[22] Taylor, 37–39.
[23] Taylor, 38.

but not under the auspices of Rome, so the institutional church of Europe fractured into Catholicism and many forms of Protestantism.

Other people, though, had had enough of Christianity altogether. They began questioning the very existence of God by denying anything beyond the material, natural universe. They swung from religious to a-religion during the Enlightenment. For these deists, agnostics, and atheists, questions about God took a backseat to the discoveries of science.

Still other people rejected both Christianity and disbelief during the Romantic era, opting to blaze new religious trails in search of a third way.[24] They couldn't shake the feeling that there was something out there beyond our ability to observe and measure through science, but it couldn't be found in traditional beliefs either. Soon, new religions sprang up left and right, like spiritualism and Christian Science.

Today, in our ever-shrinking global community, we have even *more* options—anything from major world religions, like Islam and Buddhism, to newer beliefs, like Neo-Paganism and Transhumanism.

There has been an explosion of belief in the West. Taylor attributed this to the inability of the Western mind to live under the cross pressures of belief and disbelief, the supernatural and disenchantment. Like a star collapsing under its own weight, the Western mind was compressed by these pressures until it exploded into the massive array of beliefs we see today, something Taylor called "the nova effect."[25] These alternative beliefs were slung all over our culture, and they now coexist and intermingle in our pluralistic society.

Belief in Our Pluralistic World

We no longer share a common belief system. We have options now—a lot of them. Our society is not only asking *if* we should believe in deity but *which* deity we should believe in, if we want to believe at all. There are so many options to choose from. It's hard to know which is true, if such a

---

[24] Taylor, 302.
[25] Taylor, 300.

conclusion can even be reached. We're like Sergeant James at the end of *The Hurt Locker*, who, after a year of eating the same food over and over again on military deployment, stood bewildered by the hundreds of breakfast cereal options in his local grocery. The variety is paralyzing.

What's worse is that each belief system wants us for itself, so they call to us. We are pulled from all sides to believe and disbelieve differently from the day before. Your upbringing in orthodoxy is challenged by an atheist professor, who is undermined by a Buddhist friend, who is thwarted by Jehovah's Witness missionaries, and so on.

Moreover, we don't need to look very far to find new beliefs. New beliefs find us. Friends post videos about yoga meditation and share links to UFO conspiracy sites on social media. Popular films, music, and art communicate to us on frequencies of which we are unaware. Whether we like it or not, our beliefs are always being pushed and pulled from outside forces.

And, because we can't prevent being exposed to alternatives, it's almost unthinkable that we would maintain the same belief our entire life. In fact, we tend to call unchanged people "closed-minded." The heroes of our culture aren't static in their beliefs and lifestyles. Those we admire most inherited a belief system but abandoned it, kissing faith goodbye after a quest of self-realization through the diversity of ideas. We are proud of our ideological diversity and even prouder when we change.

Our beliefs are like squares of cloth in a patchwork quilt. We deliberately pull from alternatives that are not normally related to create tailor-made worldviews. We approach belief with what Catherine Albanese called "combinativeness," the practice of combining ideas and beliefs, regardless of their origin, to create a unique, customized belief system.[26]

In years past, ideas and philosophies were kept separate from each other, neatly categorized for coherency and ease of access. Today, however, worldviews are often combinative creations, like plates at an à la carte luncheon.

---

[26] Catherine L. Albanese, *A Republic of Mind and Spirit: A Cultural History of American Metaphysical Religion* (New Haven, CT: Yale University Press, 2007), 13, 149.

We pick and choose ideas, combining what we like and discarding what we don't. We prefer it this way because it makes us feel unique and different from our peers. It doesn't really matter if I hold competing and contradicting ideas about morals, economics, and social policies. My worldview is *mine*, and it gives me a sense of uniqueness in our "age of authenticity," as Taylor put it.[27]

This is especially true as we answer the kind of questions that form our vision of fullness. Where do I come from? What is my purpose? What makes me happy? Each person answers these questions individually, assuming there is no right or wrong. In fact, it's impossible to come to a universal consensus on what's "right" or "wrong." Even those words themselves carry different meanings for different people. The words of former Supreme Court Justice Anthony Kennedy capture the American impulse for individual authenticity: "At the heart of liberty is the right to define one's own concept of existence, of meaning, of the universe, and of the mystery of human life."[28]

Truth has become relative to each person. Truth is not so much discovered as it is made.[29] Each person's "truth" is that person's own compass for right and truth or wrong and false. There is no objective set of standards under which all people live. In this kingdom of subjectivism, authenticity is king. You must live *your* truth, even if your truth contradicts the truths of other people. As Americans in this brave new world, we don't simply *pursue* happiness; it's our *right* to be happy. So, asserting your beliefs over another person's, thereby jeopardizing individual happiness, is the equivalent of ideological colonialism. You have no authority to tell others that their truth is wrong; you can only affirm personal authenticity within them and for them. In our secular culture, "equality and power [have] become the new gods,"

---

[27] Taylor, *Secular Age*, 473.

[28] Planned Parenthood v. Robert P. Casey, 505 U.S. 833 (1992).

[29] For a fascinating discussion on this topic, see Arthur Pontynen and Rod Miller, *Western Culture at the American Crossroads: Conflicts over the Nature of Science and Reason* (Wilmington, DE: Intercollegiate Studies Institute Books, 2011), 9–43.

wrote Arthur Pontynen and Rod Miller, and many people find meaning and happiness by worshiping them.[30]

So, when it comes to belief in God, who's to conclude which belief is right, if such a conclusion can be made at all? Fullness is whatever you make of it. Joy is found in that which brings you the most happiness, even if your happiness is based on what someone else would consider a lie or a vice or even harmful.

Like contestability, diversity of belief—and religious pluralism, in particular—fails to give apatheists a reason to care. Why should someone care about God if there's no consensus about *who* he is, *if* he even *is*? If I, as an apatheist, am the one who gives God meaning and I assign him none, then my indifference toward God becomes a sort of authenticity in my worldview; no one has the authority to argue otherwise.

Lacking a Reason and Lacking a Motivation

With contestability and diversity comes uncertainty, because each belief is in competition for our hearts and minds. They pull us toward themselves, constantly repositioning where we stand on issues and ideas. We experience a persistent feeling of disorientation, and no one is spared.

Atheists who are confident that the universe is just a blind, cold machine are strangely moved by the beauty of a sunset. The stunning scenery activates a longing in their souls, what John Calvin called the *sensus divinitatis*, an internal "sense of divinity [inscribed] on every heart."[31] At that moment, the atheist remembers how a Christian friend once described God as a master artist and experiences a surprising sense of transcendent sanctity. God's immanence haunts him.

Elsewhere, a Christian sitting in Philosophy 101 is exposed to the works of atheist thinkers for the first time and struggles with arguments against God's existence. It hurts their faith. God's transcendence dims in their minds.

---

[30] Pontynen and Miller, 25.

[31] John Calvin, *Institutes of the Christian Religion*, trans. Henry Beveridge (Peabody, MA: Hendrickson, 2008), 9.

In both cases, the atheist and the Christian experience uncertainty because they were exposed to different beliefs that challenged their own. So their beliefs shift a bit. The atheist's disbelief softens, and the Christian's faith weakens. And with every shift some unintended quakes must rattle the structures of our souls. Like tectonic plates deep beneath the surface of the earth, new beliefs crash and pull apart and rub against old beliefs within us, creating deep valleys of confusion and high mountains of dissonance.

As a result, our beliefs become much more fragile than before; now, they are subject to pressure from all different angles. We've lost our firm foundation. As Taylor observed, we start to believe cautiously, knowing that "a moment may come, where we no longer feel that our chosen path is compelling, or cannot justify it to ourselves or others."[32]

We don't hold to convictions as tightly as we used to, which makes our beliefs brittle. With every new exposure, we are tempted to revise our ideas about God, or, at the very least, we are aware that our views could change. Meaning and belief always feel confusing and unresolved, like a never-ending free jazz improv; that doesn't sit well with our souls.

Ornette Coleman is one of my favorite jazz musicians. Very few come close to the brightness, clarity, and originality of his instrumental voice. But there's one album of his that I can't bear to listen to. *Free Jazz* is a single-take free improvisation that sounds like eight musicians playing off eight different sheets of music all racing to see who can get to the end of the song first. Take a moment to search for it and listen. It's a great audio analogy for belief in our present age.

Imagine each instrument within *Free Jazz* as a different belief. They're all playing their own tunes at the same time. When beliefs are diverse, it's difficult to find a consistent, pleasant melody among the noise of competing voices. There are too many beliefs, too many options, too many instruments playing all at the same time.

We live in a society whose theme song is *Free Jazz*. All beliefs compete with each other to win our hearts and minds. An individual may try to keep

---

[32] Taylor, *Secular Age*, 308.

up for a while, picking out a cool melody here or a groovy drumbeat there. But, inevitably, the sax riff we enjoy is overtaken by a drum solo, which, in turn, is drowned out by a trumpet lick, and on and on.

The cacophony of *Free Jazz* is like the racket created by the many competing beliefs in our culture. We get tired of it, exhausted and irritated by the noise. So we take off our headphones and simply let go, enjoying the numbing sound of the silence found in comfort and distraction. As a nation, we've lost the reason to care about God among the discord of secularism.

In summary, some people don't care about God because they feel he isn't necessary. Science gives them all the answers to life's biggest questions. Maybe God was relevant to previous generations, but he isn't anymore. We've figured things out and feel that we no longer need him.

Other people may have cared about God at one point, but became overwhelmed at their options for belief. Maybe God exists, but who really knows? It's such a diverse and contentious issue anyway, so should a person even care?

Belief is now fractured, and we are all atomized. No two beliefs are the same, and neither do most believe very strongly (nor should we, says Rauch). Religious belief, then, has become a nebulous cloud absent of any defining features. As Steve Bruce observed, "Religion is popular in the abstract but alien in the particular," adding that, consequently, "the vast majority of the population has no knowledge of or interest in it."[33]

So, in a secular society where belief is contestable and diverse, apatheism appears because some people *lack the reason* to care about God. They either reject belief in him because of science or are demotivated by all the alternatives. But two other elements of apatheism constitute a lack of motivation to care—comfort and distraction.

---

[33] Steve Bruce, "Secularization and Its Consequences," *The Oxford Handbook on Secularism*, ed. Phil Zuckerman and John R. Shook (New York: Oxford University Press, 2017), 67.

Chapter 2 | Our Comfortable, Distracted Lives

A patheism flourishes in a secular society that is comfortable and distracted, and, of all modern nations, ours thoroughly fits this description. Perpetual advances in technology, a wealthy economy, and a stable government keep us contented and amused in ways the world has never seen. Our advanced technology offers us unparalleled convenience and entertainment.

From a small handheld device, I can order freshly prepared food delivered straight to my door while crushing digital candy and chatting with friends across the globe. The United States is an economic powerhouse that keeps us in prosperity and countless lifestyle choices. From cosplayers and salt lifers to crossfitters and online gamers, we all enjoy customized lifestyles that fit our interests and desires with like-minded communities.

And we do so safely under the protection of a government that enforces firm and fair laws while simultaneously capturing our attention with the mayhem that animates American politics. If ever there was a comfortable and distracted society, it's ours. But what do these two have to do with apathy toward God?

Belief in Our Comfortable Society

Let's consider medieval Europeans one last time. They lived very uncomfortable lives. They toiled for every meal, drudged through poverty, and felt the dangers of a hostile and unpredictable world that threatened their livelihood. From fear of thieves to disease, people lived with deep uncertainty, knowing that they might face death at any moment.

Their security of existence was often shaken, which drove them in anxiety toward what they believed brought them safety and order—God. They relied on him daily for their welfare and protection. He gave rain to the crops, protected families from robbery and death, and commanded rulers to keep order in their kingdoms. People prayed to God for good health and harvest because they had no other solutions.

But after centuries of progress, Western society made unparalleled advances. Many diseases were eradicated, wealth grew and was distributed, and governments created laws of equity that led to prosperity. The result is a very comfortable society. It's convenient, prosperous, and relatively safe.

Unlike the medievals, we rarely worry whether our needs will be met because we have ready and consistent access to food and healthcare. And we feel safe in the order and security provided by the government. Naturally, this has not always been the case, especially during times of economic recession and war. The COVID-19 pandemic of 2020, for example, exposed the fragility of our safety and prosperity in the face of global challenges. Nor is it the case the all citizens have equitable access to the same levels of health, prosperity, and safety. There are legitimate concerns about the cost of healthcare and the bewildering frequency of evils like racism and violence. We can do better, and we should. But, all things considered, at least in the United States, we typically enjoy the fruit of one of the most prosperous and powerful nations the world has ever seen.

So we pursue life, liberty, and happiness comfortably. Indeed, comfort is one of the great virtues of our society. If you're uncomfortable, then something's wrong. We hesitate to leave our comfort zones, fearful of the discomfort that inevitably follows.

And comfort is available to nearly everyone. The latest and greatest consumer goods are just a click away and delivered in mere days. Even though I could drive a few miles to the nearest grocery store to buy a ready-made meal, I don't need to. That's what food delivery services are for. Besides, I need to be at home when my monthly subscription of single-origin coffee arrives. I'll need that coffee tomorrow morning. I have an important sales pitch with a potential client. If I land it, I'll make as much money in a single day as people living three hundred years ago would make in their entire lives.

Then I can use that money to buy the latest smart home devices that automatically adjust the climate in my house, depending on my mood. Obviously, I'll want to upgrade to a security suite, which will give me peace of mind as cameras and sensors stand guard over my home. Should a robber make an attempt, I'll immediately be alerted by my phone. So will the police, and they'll dash straight over to arrest the would-be thief. And I'll watch it all go down from my phone while lying on the beach sipping my fat-free, paleo, keto-infused Frapalatté.

In this kind of world, people feel that they don't *need* God. I don't pray that God would prevent drought so my family will have grain during winter. I'm more concerned that my toddler just ordered ten boxes of cereal on my phone when I wasn't looking. I don't spend my days pleading with God to protect me from the threat of disease or war. I assume there's a vaccine and that the military is doing its job somewhere far away from home. I don't rely on God for anything. Instead, I rely on the affluence and stability of my country (or, at least, the perceived affluence and stability).

And even when life is interrupted by the threat of new disease or war, God is petitioned only for a short time until we feel that things are back within our control. At the dawn of the COVID-19 outbreak in the United States, one government official in a hard-hit region thanked God for healthcare workers and first responders on the front line.[1] They were "doing God's work" in his eyes.[2] But, just one month later, after a downward trend of

---

[1] Andrew Cuomo (@NYGovCuomo), "Thank God for our nurses, doctors and all first responders on the front line of NY's fight against #Coronavirus," Twitter, March 15, 2020, 6:41 a.m., https://twitter.com/NYGovCuomo/status /1239335925202784257.

[2] New York State Office of the Governor, "Video, Audio, Photos & Rush Transcript: Governor Cuomo: In Time of COVID-19 Pandemic, Our Healthcare Workers Are Doing 'God's Work'," news release, March 24, 2020, https://www

infection, he viewed the decline as a human achievement. "God did not stop the spread of the virus," he claimed.[3] We did.

Psychologists and sociologists have noticed this too. Researchers have long noted the relationship between mortality and belief in the supernatural, where religious belief is heightened when people come in contact with death, chaos, and uncertainty.[4]

In wealthy and stable societies, like Scandinavia, God is less important; but in impoverished parts of the world, where infant mortality and poverty are high, God is very important. Even in prosperous countries like ours, brushes with chaos and death send us running back to God. Think about how many places of worship were filled by frightened seekers in the days immediately after 9/11. During the early COVID-19 "social distancing" days, when church members stayed home and pastors live-streamed

---

.governor.ny.gov/news/video-audio-photos-rush-transcript-governor-cuomo -time-covid-19-pandemic-our-healthcare-workers.

[3] Adrienne Vogt, "New York Governor Says 'Phased Reopening' of the State Will Take Months," CNN, April 14, 2020, https://edition.cnn.com /world/live-news/coronavirus-pandemic-intl-04-14-20/h_3bed58b8faba8edcf e5955201319934a.

[4] Mark Dechesne et al., "Literal and Symbolic Immortality: The Effect of Evidence of Literal Immortality on Self-Esteem Striving in Response to Mortality Salience," *Journal of Personality & Social Psychology* 84 (2003): 722–37; Ara Norenzayan and Ian G. Hansen, "Belief in Supernatural Agents in the Face of Death," *Personality and Social Psychology Bulletin* 32 (2006): 174–87; Kenneth E. Vail III et al., "A Terror Management Analysis of the Psychological Functions of Religion," *Personality and Social Psychology Review* 14 (2010): 84–94; Aaron C. Kay et al., "Randomness, Attributions of Arousal, and Belief in God," *Psychological Science* 21 (2010): 216–18; Aaron C. Kay et al., "Religious Belief as Compensatory Control," *Personality and Social Psychology Review* 14 (2010), 37–48; Bastiaan T. Rutjens et al., "Deus or Darwin: Randomness and Belief in Theories about the Origin of Life," *Journal of Experimental Social Psychology* 46 (2010): 1078–80; Kenneth E. Vail III et al., "Exploring the Existential Function of Religion and Supernatural Agent Beliefs among Christians, Muslims, Atheists, and Agnostics," *Personality and Social Psychology Bulletin* 38 (2012): 1288–1300; Jonathan Jong et al., "Foxhole Atheism, Revisited: The Effects of Mortality Salience on Explicit and Implicit Religious Belief," *Journal of Experimental Social Psychology* 48 (2012): 983–89.

sermons, there was a noticeable increase in overall views, at least in my experience. As long as we feel safe and stable, God is less likely to play a role in our lives. When we have a sense of existential security, a feeling of whole safety in body and mind, there's no need for God, so he becomes irrelevant.

Psychologists Will Gervais and Ara Norenzayan argued that apatheism grows from "conditions of existential security."[5] Such conditions include lower poverty rates, decreased infant mortality, longer lifespans, economic stability, and reliable government services and social safety nets.

They concluded, "Where life is safe and predictable, people are less motivated to turn to gods for succor."[6] In other words, the more a society feels safe and taken care of, the less important it finds God to be. And the less motivated people are to turn to God, the less likely they will find his existence relevant. After all, why concern yourself with God if you feel secure in body, mind, and soul without him?

In a comfortable and safe society like ours, apatheists lack the *motivation* to care about God.

Belief in Our Distracted Society

"Busy." That's my default answer when people ask how I am. "It's a *good* busy, though," I justify myself, adding something about idle hands and the devil. I like to think my life is so busy because I'm accomplishing a lot. But that's only true if by "accomplishments" I mean staying current on breaking news and trending hashtags.

With smartphone in hand, from sunrise to sunset, the one thing that captures my attention is everything. During my morning coffee, I open my Bible app to pick up where I last left off, but my finger is diverted by red bubbles and white numbers that hover over my favorite apps. They're luring me into a time trap, and, more often than not, the temptation wins my attention.

---

[5] Ara Norenzayan and Will M. Gervais, "The Origins of Religious Disbelief," *Trends in Cognitive Sciences* 17 (2013): 21–22.

[6] Norenzayan and Gervais, 22.

The next thing I know, fifteen minutes have passed, and I'm engrossed in a Wikipedia article on the assassination of Archduke Franz Ferdinand. Why? I don't know, nor do I remember how I even got there. What I do know, however, is that the comfort offered by our modern world also brings with it a nearly unavoidable distraction.

Email alerts. Text messages. Notifications. Ads and pop-ups. They've all trained my brain to redistribute my limited focus across a thousand things at once. I check my stock portfolio during church meetings. I listen to podcasts while feeding my infant. I stream sitcoms while preparing dinner. When I lose cell reception, I feel disoriented and anxious.

I'm old enough to remember when the world wasn't so distracting, when summers were filled with one goal—escaping boredom. Sure, we had amusing video games and played them often, but not as often as we played neighborhood-wide capture-the-flag or baseball in the sandlot.

I also remember when email moved from the workplace into homes and when social media was born. The idea was to make communication with colleagues and friends easier and more convenient to increase efficiency at work, thus affording us more time for family and play at home.

If you wanted to access email and social media, then you needed the investment of a personal computer and the Internet, neither of which was cheap. Then you'd need to sign on to services like AOL and Myspace. You'd turn on the computer, join the Internet (which took a few minutes, and could only be accomplished if Mom wasn't already on the phone), and log in to check your messages. These services couldn't come to you. They were locked behind stationary processes that took time and effort to open. It was cumbersome, so you'd only check them a few times each week.

But something changed. The Internet became faster and more afford-able as it migrated from PCs to smart phones. Bulky, expensive software shrank into free apps that alert us with dings and chimes all day long on mobile devices. We no longer go to apps; apps come to us. And every time they do, our attention gets diverted. We tried to adapt by multitasking, and digital natives of younger generations are said to do it best. But there's no such thing as true multitasking when it comes to contemplation and meditation. I'm a millennial, the son of a computer engineer, and I can't multitask for anything, especially not volleying my attention back and forth between Scripture and screens.

In the modern world, it feels nearly impossible to meditate on any one thing at a time. This includes the most worthy object of our meditation—God.

Too Distracted to Think about God

Alan Noble woke me up to this crisis of distraction in our secular age. In *Disruptive Witness*, he argued that the persistent distraction of our culture prevents us from asking the deepest, most important questions about existence and truth. The things that prick our souls for the sake of the gospel (e.g., death, beauty, anxiety, etc.) can be numbed quickly by an eight-hour dose of binge-watching *The Office*. We effortlessly avoid asking the biggest, most difficult questions of life because we are so busy.

This is especially true in America, where we find personal value in what we produce. The more things we can do in a day, the more valuable we feel. Technology gives us thousands of tasks to accomplish, from replying to emails to playing mobile games. With every click of the send button and point earned toward the next level, we feel like we're making real progress toward some actual goal. And the newer the goal via the newest media, the better. "We are addicted to novelty," Noble observed, "and as with most addictions, it takes a toll on our bodies: we become mentally fatigued, 'scrambled.'"[7]

So we lose our ability to focus on what matters most. Consequently, Noble lamented, "The modern mind is often not prepared to engage in dialogue about personally challenging ideas, particularly ones with deep implications."[8] We have too many tasks, too many goals, and most of them

---

[7] Alan Noble, *Disruptive Witness: Speaking Truth in a Distracted Age* (Downers Grove, IL: InterVarsity Press, 2018), 21.

[8] Noble, 21.

are irrelevant to the most important stuff of life. We lack the bandwidth for self-reflection.

Worse yet, even if we wanted to siphon time for introspection, we struggle to tell the difference between what matters most and what doesn't matter at all. "The space between the trivial and the crucial has shrunk," Noble pointed out. "Everything is important all of the time, and you are obligated to keep up."[9] In this task-oriented world, it's just as important to us that we respond to the latest celebrity faux pas on Twitter as it is to pray over our children before we put them to bed.

Technology hasn't given us more freedom to rest; it's demanded more of us all the time. And we stick with it because technology gives us a false sense of meaning. As Noble argued, it "gives us the sense that we are tapped into something greater than ourselves."[10] We offer the world a curated version of our lives and, in exchange, the world assesses our value with hearts, upvotes, and retweets. So we continue feeding into technology because we think it's giving us happiness and a sense of meaning, but it's not. There's a cheesy word for this: "appiness," the fleeting feeling of euphoria we get from the apps on our phone. Meaning ought to come from something that transcends the world, not something that incessantly exposes us to the millions of competing "meanings" available through lifestyles, shopping, politics, and play.

Even if we wanted to discover some greater meaning beyond technology, we're swimming upstream. Our brains have been rewired to value what's fast and immediate rather than slow and eventual. We want everything right here and now. If an idea cannot be communicated in a meme or a 280-character Tweet, then it's not worth our time.

But you can't microwave personal formation, which is why Christianity values calm and quiet practices that draw us in slowly over extended seasons of spiritual formation and internalizing truth. It advocates for Sabbath, prayer, meditation, reflection, and study. Our society, however, prefers a quicker avenue. In the time we listen to a sermon on one passage of one

---

[9] Noble, 23.
[10] Noble, 15.

book of the Bible, we could have watched three or four TED talks about multiple subjects. The Bible feels outdated—it's much quicker to do an Internet search than to read, study, and meditate on an ancient book. And why pray for wisdom when you can YouTube the advice you seek?

Christianity in our digital age calls for something radically different. Our faith invites us to do things more slowly while the world offers us quicker. It's true what they say—time is a commodity in the modern world. Most of us have bankrupted ourselves by spreading our attention so thin across multiple platforms that it's almost unthinkable to devote hours to sermon listening, Scripture reading, and prayer. Belief in God feels so old and out-of-date.

But technology alone is not driving our busyness. There is something hidden deep in my response of "busy" to the question "How are you?" I am doing more than I should because I want to feel like I am valuable. Our culture promotes a relentless drive to achieve the American dream by making improvements that lead to accomplishments. The best of us are always killing it at work because we equate who we *are* with what we *do*. We are busy *being*, not merely *doing*.

To be busy communicates importance. To be accomplished means we are needed. And we think that to be important and needed brings us happiness, so happiness is ultimately found in what we do. Happiness, like truth, is manufactured. Our whole identities become wrapped up in what we do. This is why the first question we ask strangers at parties is, "What do you do for a living?" We're gauging one another's value and worth, whether we know it or not. If God cannot help us rank up in our careers or social statuses, then he is irrelevant to our pursuit of fullness through doing.

In this distracted world, God isn't merely unneeded, he's *unnoticed*. There simply isn't time to think about something that we doubt exists, is too diverse in options, and doesn't seem necessary. Besides, even if we want to contemplate belief in God, to concentrate long enough to pick out a pleasing melody in the "free jazz" of belief, we can't. Our attention has become too divided.

So, who has the attention span or time to care about God? Aren't there more pressing things to think about? Some apatheists simply have no motivation to care.

Lacking the Will to Care about God

In our secular, comfortable, and distracted age, it's easy to be indifferent to God. Belief in the supernatural is no longer taken for granted; we're all a bit skeptical now. But belief in God hasn't disappeared. Instead, faith and skepticism live side by side, joined by countless alternative beliefs. Sometimes God is part of these beliefs, but other times he's not. For many people, there isn't any incentive to ensure that he's part of their belief. Our affluence provides all we need, so we don't feel God is necessary. Besides, in our distracted lifestyles, most rarely even notice him.

It's in this soil—contestability, diversity, comfort, and distraction—that apatheism not only grows but flourishes. These four factors account for the two primary reasons apatheism exists. First, people *lack a reason* to care about God because of secularism, and second, people *lack the motivation* to care about God because of affluence and technology.

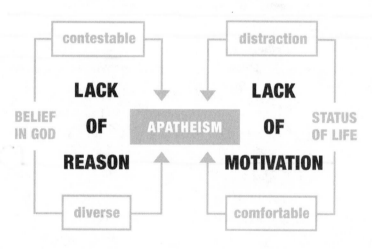

Figure 2.1

Apatheism can occur when someone lacks the reason to care about God because of secularism (i.e., the contestability and diversity of belief). Apatheism can also occur when someone lacks the motivation to care about God because of comfort and distraction.

This doesn't mean that caring about God in our age of apathy is impossible. Someone who wanted to care could find the right reasons and motivation. Secularism, comfort, and distraction aren't insurmountable obstacles. There are plenty of reasons to believe in God and the supernatural rather than a cold, material cosmos without transcendent meaning or purpose. It's possible to get off the couch and enter into uncomfortable situations that challenge assumptions and lifestyles. Technology can be turned off for a season so that meditation on the big questions becomes possible.

Lacking the reason and motivation to care about God is more an excuse than a limitation. Such excuses can only hold us captive if we let them, and we stay in their captivity because we want to.

I can't run a marathon, at least not at the moment. The reason I can't endure a long-distance run is that I'm not in the proper shape to do so, but this is also my excuse. The difference between my ability and inability to run a marathon isn't actually my fitness; it's ultimately a matter of my will. I don't *want* to run that long.

Likewise, some people don't *want* to know God truly and love him fully—they lack the will to care; they are overwhelmed with reasons to be indifferent.

I can't help but think about the story of Jesus's encounter with the rich young ruler (Matt 19:16–22; Mark 10:17–22; Luke 18:18–23). That young man lived a comfortable, wealthy lifestyle. I have no doubt he'd have appeared in the *Jerusalem Tribune's* "Top 30 under 30" that year. From the perspective of the ruler, he was fine with Jesus when it came to following the law and being a good person (although, of course, we know he wasn't). Religion for him was a means to an end, a way to learn the right deeds that lead to fulfillment. But he still felt like he was coming up short, like he lacked something.

So he found Jesus and asked what additional religious deeds he ought to do. What the man needed, though, wasn't religion; he needed righteousness, a righteousness that can only come from God himself by faith. The cost of that righteousness turned out to be obedience and conformity to the pattern Christ sets before us. Jesus instructed the ruler to sell everything he had, give it to the poor, and follow him.

But that cost was too high—he loved his wealth so much that he couldn't love Jesus more. Could he have loved Jesus more than his wealth? Of course, but he didn't want to. So the ruler walked away from true joy.

Similarly, some apatheists love their lives the way they are because they offer them some form of authenticity and fullness. But that fullness isn't actually *full*. They sense there is something more. So they search for what they're missing. When they find the answer—when they encounter God— they recognize there's a cost associated with the fullness he offers. They'll need to change by sacrificing their lifestyles and following God's Son. But that's too high a cost, so they employ apathy to shield themselves from disappointment. Like the fox who couldn't reach the grapes, apatheists didn't really want God anyway.

This kind of apathy exists because we live in an age of "authenticity" that encourages us to craft individual identities based on picking and choosing what we want to believe. We evaluate beliefs not so much based on right or wrong, whether something is true or false. Rather, we accept or reject them based on whether or not they will benefit us, especially as we build our authentic selves and project them to the world. And the purpose of this self-building is to discover fullness.

So, as a whole, we are less interested in veracity than utility. Unless a belief is seen as complementing and improving a person's individual self, it's tossed aside. Unless Jesus can add eternal life to our wealthy lifestyle, he's not worth following.

For apatheists, whether or not God exists and has revealed himself through Jesus Christ is far less important than whether Christianity helps or hinders the people they want to become. If their authentic selves are marked by some kind of moral piety, then, sure, Christianity might help. But if they're trying to develop *personas* incompatible with Christian beliefs, then Christianity is of no help to them. Or if they're comfortable with who they are and Christianity is asking them to change, they don't want it. They prefer tranquility over truth.[11] If belief in God doesn't improve the lives they want to live, it's not "their truth," and neither do they want it to be.

This is, I believe, the core reason why apatheism exists—we do not *want* to care about God. We've developed an antipathy toward spiritual contemplation because we don't want what inevitably follows, a fundamental change in who we are and how we live. To sacrifice autonomy is too high a cost, so we protect it through apathy.

Summary

Apatheism occurs when someone thinks and feels God is unimportant. In short, apatheism exists because people lack the reason, motivation, and will to care about God. He's not needed to explain why we're here; science has given us the answer. Besides, which version of God in the multitude of beliefs leads to truth anyway? He's unnecessary for our fulfillment; happiness is found in affluence and our distracted pursuit of meaning. When it's all said and done, apatheists don't want to care because their wants have been trained to look elsewhere for meaning and joy.

---

[11] Douglas Groothuis, "Why Truth Matters: An Apologetic for Truth-Seeking in Postmodern Times," *Journal of the Evangelical Theological Society* 47 (2004): 450. Concerning this point, Groothuis further argued that apatheism excludes "in principle the discovery of and adherence to any truths not found comfortable by people who place tranquility above reality."

Chapter 3 | Exploring Apatheism in Detail

I met Chris at a community gathering for kayakers. There are a lot of us where I live, a port city nestled on a large bay. Inevitably, at these kinds of gatherings, what I do for a living comes up in conversation.

"A pastor? That's cool," Chris said unconvincingly.

"What about you?" I asked. I was inquiring about his work, but he misunderstood me.

"Well, religion isn't really my thing."

Once you tell people that you're a pastor, spirituality colors the conversation. So, I pressed into it.

"Why's that? If you don't mind me asking."

Chris then relayed a story that's becoming increasingly common—a "faith journey" from fervent belief to apatheism.

He was born into a Pentecostal family, surrounded by people whose unwavering commitment to religious belief made God feel very real. Chris was passionate about God, having surrendered his life to Christ at a summer camp in response to an altar call. There was even talk that he might head off to Bible college to become a pastor. But after receiving a sports scholarship, he attended a local state university. There, he made new friends among his teammates. They were not at all like the church community in his hometown. In a matter of weeks, he walked away from the piety of his youth, finding happiness in the pleasures of the party scene. Chris believed in God, but his belief didn't affect his life.

Chris became a practical atheist. It's *practical* atheism, not *actual* atheism, because unlike atheism proper, practical atheists merely act as if God does not exist and has no authority over their lives, despite believing in and caring about God's existence.

Then something changed for Chris. He took a philosophy course taught by an atheist professor that completely fractured his faith. He consumed books on a-religious skepticism, from the works of Voltaire and Nietzsche to popular books by New Atheists like Richard Dawkins and Christopher Hitchens. For months, his spare time was exhausted watching debates online and attending the university's secular student club. His passion for God transformed into passion against God. Chris no longer believed in God, but he also hated him.

This heated skepticism cost him. His believing parents all but shunned him; his friends from high school wanted nothing to do with him. The coldness he received pushed him deeper into his atheism. It made him angrier.

Eventually, Chris felt he could no longer pay the high cost of his fury. He still disbelieved, but he didn't feel as strongly about his disbelief. His atheism didn't evaporate; it cooled. And he's never really believed very strongly one way or another since.

There were times when he revisited his old beliefs in God, but they faded quickly. He claimed that Christians were too hypocritical and judgmental, so he reasoned that their beliefs must be the root cause. For Chris, neither the evidence for faith nor the examples he'd seen were sufficient to persuade him to believe again. He became an incredulous agnostic, someone who refuses to commit to belief one way or another because of an apparent lack of credible evidence to believe, especially displays of faith from believers.

Later in life, he met his future wife, Paige, at a work event. Her love for meditation drew him into Buddhism. Maybe the God of Christianity doesn't exist, but perhaps something transcendent does. Immanence pulled Chris back from the materialism cliff. And maybe while he felt the Christians he knew didn't model their beliefs very well, he thought that his

Buddhist friends lived out their beliefs. He found displays of religion that made Buddhism seem credible.[1]

By then, he was ready to give religion another chance, but he wouldn't be so emotionally invested this time around. He believed that strong feelings for and against God were two sides of the same coin. They both took belief too seriously, which had gotten him into unnecessary arguments that scarred his most valued relationships. Besides, the world itself could do with a little more peace, and that starts with setting down tired arguments about religion.

He then told me how the years had passed, and that, after a while, he and his wife started having kids. By the time the children reached school age, Chris and Paige felt the need to teach their children virtues and values. So their kids were enrolled in a mainline Protestant private school. A year or so later, the whole family found themselves in the pews, attending once a month or so. Religion was good for his young children. One day, though, they'd need to make their own choices. If they choose to stay with Christianity, that's fine. If not, that's okay, too.

Toward the end of the conversation, I wanted to know where exactly Chris's beliefs lay today, so I asked: "What do you believe about God now?"

He paused for a moment as if he had not considered the question in a while. "You know," he said, "I guess I just don't care." He smiled. "Is that terrible to say?" He then made clear that he personally believes in some kind of divinity, but that belief isn't crucial to his life.

"And church? Is there anything about God that drew you back in?" I asked.

He said that what attracted him to church and the Buddhist meditation center wasn't God, but the happiness and community that they brought him and his family. Even then, he's not all that committed to the church.

---

[1] See Joseph Henrich, "The Evolution of Costly Displays, Cooperation and Religion: Credibility Enhancing Displays and Their Implications for Cultural Evolution," *Journal of Evolution and Human Behavior* 30 (2009): 244–60. Henrich called this "credibility-enhancing display" of faith.

"In fact, I don't consider myself a Christian. It's more like being spiritual without the organized religion," he explained. Sociologists would classify Chris as part of the ever-growing "Nones," those who have no religious affiliation, despite attending religious services or even holding some religious beliefs. To me, he's less a None than he is a Some, combining *some* beliefs without actually holding any that could be classified in traditional ways. He's a type of Albanese's "combinative" believer.

In the end, Chris had hiked all across the continent of belief on his faith journey. He's exhausted, having propped up his feet to rest after a long trek from fundamentalism to practical atheism to New Atheism to incredulous agnosticism to Buddhism to Buddhism-practicing, Episcopalian apatheism.

He finds happiness in his paddling lifestyle, out on the water among the waves and dolphins. He's an apatheist now, exhausted from listening to the confusing noise of different voices competing for his heart and mind.

"So," Chris concluded his story, "what kind of kayak do you own?"

He ended his story back where we began—talking about kayaks. He's not interested in my faith. It's fine that I believe, but he doesn't care. He's all about the paddling lifestyle, distracted by the sea in the comfort of his kayak. He's passionate about his community, pursuing fullness with the people who accompany his favorite pastime.

How Apatheism Affects Us

Do you know someone like Chris? Nowadays, I think it's safe to say that most of us do. It's a complicated journey that began with passion for God, but after, wading through a plethora of ideas and emotions, has ended—or, at least, is temporarily resting—in apatheism.

There's a listlessness about such belief, a lack of concern and interest for something worthy of our utmost affection and attention. This is how apatheism affects us. Indifference saturates every square inch of how we think and feel about God.

For Chris, apatheism has rendered faith useless. He doesn't find God all that interesting because he doesn't believe that God is important. He's thought it through, even tried on different beliefs to see how they feel. But in the end, belief seems irrational, inconsistent, and useless to him. So, he thinks little about the idea of God. He has no cognitive aspiration to view the world in light of a transcendent Creator who is providentially involved in his life. He's rationally indifferent to God.

At the core of apatheism is indifference to questions related to God's existence.[2] I like to call these "God questions": Does God exist? Can we know if God exists? If so, how does he reveal himself, and what is he like? What is the nature of his person and character? And what does God do? If God does not exist, then what does his non-existence mean?

I asked Chris a couple of these God questions. He responded with shrugged shoulders. An apatheist is not just indifferent to the answers we have for these questions, but (this is *very* important) also to the questions themselves. This indifference makes an apatheist very distinct from other folks we might intuitively lump together, like atheists and agnostics. Apatheism is *not* agnosticism or atheism, although an agnostic or atheist can be apatheistic. Let me explain.

Philosopher Milenko Budimir noticed how apatheistic indifference distinguishes apatheism from these different positions. He observed:

> Classical theism is the position that a god or gods exist. In contrast, atheism argues that a god or gods do not exist. Lastly, there is agnosticism which holds that there is just not enough evidence to prove or disprove the existence of a god. Now apatheism is the

---

[2] Robert Nash, *Religious Pluralism in the Academy: Opening the Dialogue* (New York: Peter Lang, 2001), 27. Nash first noted how apatheism is, at its core, apathy toward questions related to God's existence or nonexistence. Subsequently, philosophers Trevor Hedberg and Jordan Huzarevich paired apatheism with "existence questions" in their defense of apatheism, "Appraising Objections to Practical Apatheism." *Philosophia* 45 (2017): 257–76. I prefer the term "God questions" over "existence questions" because apatheism moves beyond mere indifference toward God's existence into related topics concerning his person, character, and actions, and our relation to him.

position that whether or not a god exists is just not that important
of a question, that it has little relevancy.[3]

In other words, a theist *believes* that God exists; an atheist *believes* God
doesn't exist; an agnostic believes that we *can't know* whether or not God
exists; but an apatheist *doesn't care* whether or not God exists. This is why,
as a Christian, you can have a meaningful and lively conversation about
God questions with an atheist but not with an apatheist. Even though atheists answer God questions in the negative, at least they care about them.
Apatheists couldn't care less because they *feel* nothing about God questions.

Jonathan Rauch, a self-described atheistic apatheist, captured this dis-
tinction between apatheism and atheism when he noticed that apatheism
"concerns not *what* you believe but *how*."[4] He described apatheism as "a
disinclination to care all that much about one's own religion, and an even
stronger disinclination to care about other people's [religion]."[5] Notice how
apatheism seeps into the heart, affecting not only our beliefs but also our
emotions. We shouldn't merely *think* religion is unimportant—we shouldn't
care at all.

Why? Because God isn't necessary nowadays, so he has little (if anything)
to do with the things we care most about in life. Do I have meaning? What
kind of person should I be? Which causes should I support? Whom should
I befriend, date, or marry? What lifestyle will bring me happiness? God is
absent as a factor for consideration in every one of these questions. Instead,
we look to the earthly sources immediately before us—like ourselves, others,
and things—to aid us in achieving self-realization, our fulfillment.

Caring involves more than what we think; caring involves how we feel
and act and live. So it's no surprise that apatheism manifests itself as an
attitude of disinterest. In fact, that's the primary way we know someone is
apatheistic. People's thoughts are invisible, but the blasé, disinterested look on

---

[3] Milenko Budimir, "Apatheism: The New Face of Religion?" *Philosophy of Religion* 45 (2008), 88–93.

[4] Rauch, "Let It Be," 34–35 (see chap. 1, n. 13). Emphasis added.

[5] Rauch, 34–35.

their faces isn't. Their holistic apathy toward God—both mind and heart—is what philosopher Gabriel Citron calls *theapathy*, the state of being completely apathetic or indifferent toward God.[6] Apatheism manifests itself as theapathy. If a person does not believe God is important (apathe*ism*), then, naturally, he will express apathy toward God (theapathy). In short, apatheism is when a person believes that God is unimportant and feels that way as well. So an apatheist is cognitively indifferent *and* emotionally apathetic toward God.

The Duality of Apatheism

There is a duality to apatheism—belief *and* behavior, mind *and* heart, cognition *and* affection. Apatheism is much more than the *-ism* implies. It's not just a mental position; it's also an orientation of the heart. This is a crucial point to understand because human beings aren't merely *Homo sapiens*.

What I mean is that we are more than "man" (*homo*) who thinks or reasons (*sapiens*). As creatures created in the image of the triune God revealed in creation and Scripture, we are fundamentally *Homo imago*, "man who images." Scripture teaches us that all humans were created in God's image with the capacity to know him and the inclination to love him (Gen 1:26–28). Like a child knows and loves his or her father, so we were all created to know and to love our heavenly Father, which is why Adam (whose name means "man") is described as the "son of God" (Luke 3:38). We are the "glory of God" when we enter into and act in that familial relationship (1 Cor 11:7). No wonder part of the Greatest Commandment is to love the Lord God with "all your heart, with all your soul, and with all your mind" (Matt 22:37).

It isn't that I think, therefore I am. I image, therefore I am. The Enlightenment vision of being human assumes the distinguishing marker between humanity and animals is our ability to outthink the rest of the animal kingdom. But we are much more than thinking things, or, as

---

[6] Gabriel Citron, "Theapathy & Theaffectivity: On (Not) Caring about God," unpublished paper received in communication with the author, November 19, 2018.

philosopher James K. A. Smith put it, we aren't simply "brains-on-a-stick."[7] We learn and act with our whole being, and our hearts play a more significant role in this than we realize. We are "first and foremost *lovers*," Smith argued, beings who think *and* feel, who know *and* desire.[8] Our minds and hearts are inseparably linked. So thoughts of indifference about God lead to feelings of apathy toward him, and vice versa. This is one reason that the Greatest Commandment pairs love with both our hearts *and* minds. To love God is to think highly of him, and to think highly of God is to love him. A believer who thinks often of God's faithfulness will have great affection toward him, and her affection will only increase her high respect of God. But the opposite is also true. To be apathetic toward God is to think indifferently about him, and vice versa. Apatheists who believe God isn't all that important are unlikely to exhibit any affection toward him, and a cold heart toward God feeds into their attitude of indifference.

What and How We Think

It seems counterintuitive that *how* we feel about something can affect *what* we think, but it happens all the time. I'll never forget the first time I encountered a bear in the wild. I was visiting a friend in Montana and decided to go on a hike alone while he was at work. After a few hours in, far from the trailhead and any other person, I heard heavy footsteps in the forest behind me. When I stopped to listen, so did the footsteps. As I started to walk again, the footsteps returned. I stopped, turned around, and looked intently into the woods.

That's when I heard it—the low, muffled growl that sent a chill down my spine. Everything in me at that moment told me to run, but I decided to stand still. I could see furry black shoulder blades through the branches, but nothing more. Fortunately, it wasn't all that interested and let me walk (very cautiously) away.

---

[7] James K. A. Smith, *You Are What You Love: The Spiritual Power of Habit* (Grand Rapids: Brazos Press, 2016), 3.

[8] Smith, 7.

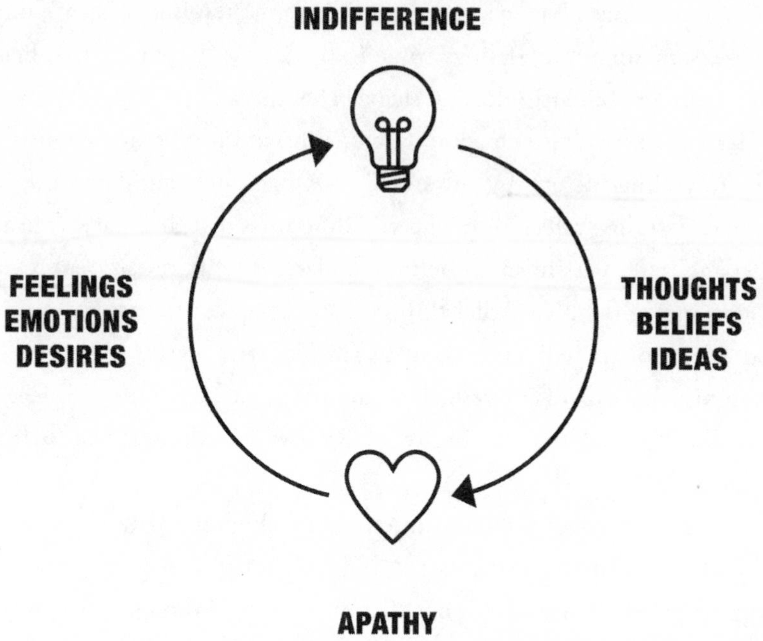

INDIFFERENCE

FEELINGS
EMOTIONS
DESIRES

THOUGHTS
BELIEFS
IDEAS

APATHY

Figure 3.1
Apathy toward God is both a heart and a mind issue.
Our thoughts and beliefs about God affect our hearts, and our
feelings and emotions toward God affect our minds.

Reflecting on that episode, I remember experiencing two reactions. The first was a primal reaction of fear. The second was a rational reaction of interest. My gut reaction told me to flee immediately. It was a self-preserving sensation that nearly overtook my thoughts about the situation. My rational response, though, wanted to know what kind of bear it was and to strategize my safest move. It was a curiosity that took note of the bear's size and color, and a recollection of all the episodes of *Alone* I watched to remember how the contestants dealt with bears.

In that moment, I experienced both rational and emotional responses to what I saw. My emotions grabbed my rationality by the collar, pulled my mind close, and screamed, "Run, fool!" But I stayed calm. The emotional nearly took control until the rational wrestled it into submission.

Our emotions and feelings are not always the result of what we think; instead, sometimes our feelings come first and our thinking later.[9] Beliefs shape attitudes, but attitudes also shape beliefs.

It's not difficult to imagine how cognitive indifference about God leads to feelings of apathy toward him. A hardened mind toward God can have a dulling effect on the heart. Sometimes disbelief leads to heated anger and fierce pessimism. A definite undercurrent of resentment toward religion moves the New Atheist movement: a pugnacious attitude against God is one of its hallmarks. But disbelief doesn't always lead to anger. It can also lead to disinterest. The same arguments against God's existence that ignited the popularity of Richard Dawkins can also foster nonchalance.

On the other hand, it's also true that a feeling of apathy toward God can lead to cognitive indifference. A dulled heart toward God has a hardening effect on the mind. It's not that all apatheists thought their way to theapathy. Just the opposite—they felt nothing for God first and are now uninterested in God questions.

This is an important point to make because it shapes how we understand and approach apatheism. If apatheism is merely a matter of the mind, then the problem lies with beliefs; if apatheism is a matter of the heart, then the problem lies with disordered affections.

But if apatheism is a matter of both the heart and the mind, then we need to develop a holistic approach that confronts apathy both intellectually *and* emotionally. And that begins with a proper perspective on not just *what* we believe but also *how* we believe.

---

[9] Iain McGilchrist, *The Master and His Emissary: The Divided Brain and the Making of the Western World* (New Haven, CT: Yale University Press, 2009), 184. McGilchrist, a psychiatrist, put it this way: "One's feelings are not a reaction to, or a superposition on, one's cognitive assessment, but the reverse: the affect comes first, the thinking later."

What and How We Believe

We tend to conceptualize belief in God as merely the sum of our ideas concerning him. If you believe God exists, then you're a theist. If you don't, then you're an atheist. If you're not sure, then you're agnostic. Our thoughts are plotted along a spectrum of supernaturalism and naturalism (see fig. 3.2). Every belief is positioned somewhere along this line. On one far side is theism. On the other is atheism. In the middle are varying levels of uncertainty.

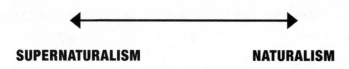

SUPERNATURALISM   **NATURALISM**

Figure 3.2

This is how pollsters gauge belief in society.[10] Sociologists conduct massive surveys to determine the frequency and diversity of religion by asking people what they believe. For example, the Pew Research Center asks questions like "Do you believe in God or a universal spirit?" and "How certain are you about this belief?"[11] Their concern is the content and certainty of belief. Christians and Muslims end up on the far side of supernaturalism. Agnostics are somewhere in the middle. Skeptics and atheists hang out toward the side of naturalism. Whether or not they will slide from

---

[10] One example of an exception to this norm is a 2016 poll from PRRI that addressed apatheism specifically. It defined an apatheist as someone for whom "religion is not personally important to them, but believe it generally is more socially helpful than harmful." Betsy Cooper, Daniel Cox, Rachel Lienesch, and Robert P. Jones, *Exodus: Why Americans are Leaving Religion—and Why They're Unlikely to Come Back* (Washington, DC: Public Religion Research Institute, 2016), 13.

[11] Pew Research Center, "2014 Religious Landscape Study," May 30, 2014, https://www.pewforum.org/wp-content/uploads/sites/7/2015/11/201.11.03_rls_ii_questionnaire.pdf.

supernaturalism to naturalism relies on the certainty of their beliefs. If they are sure about what they believe—if they have firm *ideas* backed by satisfactory *reason*—then they will likely stay put.

But this method doesn't capture the whole story. It only speaks to *what* is believed, not *how* it is believed. There is a world of difference in the intensity of theism between Billy Graham and a nominal Catholic just as there is between the atheism of Richard Dawkins and Jonathan Rauch, the atheistic apatheist mentioned earlier. Simply because you believe that there is a God does not necessarily mean you are concerned about him, and if you do not believe in God, it's not always the case that you are indifferent toward him.

Belief in God, then, is better thought of as existing on a plane of two axes measuring the type and intensity of belief. The X axis of this plane is *what* we believe; the Y axis is how we *feel* about our beliefs. What we believe oscillates between supernaturalism and naturalism, and how we believe fluctuates between fervor and apathy. The more strongly we feel about our belief, whether it's supernatural or not, the closer we approach fervor. The less intensely we feel about belief, the closer we come to apathy. At some point, the nearer we draw to apathy, the more we enter into apatheism, regardless of whether or not we believe in God (see fig. 3.3).

Apatheism can be both religious and a-religious. Someone may believe in God but not care about that belief. Another person might disbelieve in God but not care about that disbelief. In other words, it's equally possible to believe in God and not care about him and to disbelieve in God and not care about him, i.e., theistic apatheism and atheistic apatheism. Sure, there are apatheists among skeptics, but there are also apatheists in the pews.

Consider Chris's journey (see fig. 3.4). He began in Pentecostal fundamentalism with all the certainty and fervor toward God one can muster. God existed—that much was obvious. And God was extremely active in his life, so Chris responded in fervor. He attended church and Bible studies multiple times a week, spent weekends practicing door-to-door evangelism, and continually chose faith over friendships in school, even though it cost him. Chris began his faith journey very high along the axes of supernaturalism and fervor.

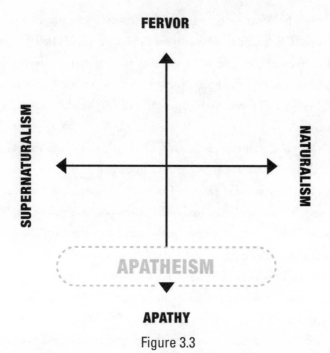

Figure 3.3

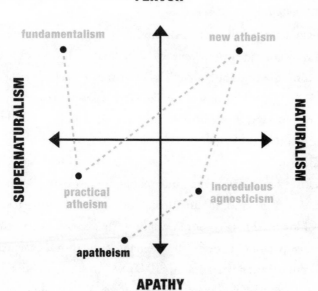

Figure 3.4

But then he went to college and befriended teammates who liked to party. Slowly, Chris let go of his zeal for God, but not his belief. Over a year or so, his affection for God slipped down toward apathy, even though his belief in God never really changed. He became a practical atheist, someone who still believed in God (high supernaturalism) but didn't act accordingly (low fervor).

Then came the atheist professor who convinced Chris that God didn't exist and that religion was dangerous. Chris's belief swung radically to disbelief, and his fervor was reignited. Only this time, his passion was set against God. Skepticism animated him. Instead of church and Bible studies, he attended lectures and meetings at the secular student union. He became the opposite of an evangelist as he tried to unconvert believers, especially Christians. And his fiery skepticism cost him relationships.

But after a while, he let go of his anger. He became an incredulous agnostic, still unwilling to believe faithfully but also not willing to disbelieve entirely. His passion was a bit more tempered—God was somewhat important, just not *that* important. Until he saw credible evidence of God's existence in the lives of believers, he wasn't going to concern himself all that much with religion.

His wife changed that when she and her meditation center gave Chris what he was looking for—people who, at least in his mind, walked the walk. To him, the Buddhists practiced what they preached, so he was willing to believe again that something like God exists. By that point, though, whether or not God exists became irrelevant. He didn't care. He slipped into apatheism, even though he held some religious views that he learned from Buddhism.

Belief is more dynamic than mere thoughts and ideas. Belief animates, moves, and stirs us. And, in our stirring, our hearts affect what we believe. Feelings of love and hate color our opinions. It seems counterintuitive, but apatheism is dynamic. Beneath the stagnant layers of nonchalance runs an active current between heart and mind. So, we must remember this moving forward: for an apatheist, the gospel isn't necessarily an invitation to shift toward theism on the spectrum of belief; it's an invitation to rise from indifference toward affection for Love itself.

Who Isn't an Apatheist?

Apatheists are all around us. Some of them you know from work, others from university. A few of them might even be from your church. Someone can claim to be a Christian and be an apatheist at the same time. But it's worth mentioning that not all apathy in the church is apatheism and, if we're not careful, we risk misdiagnosing a close cousin of apatheism—"practical atheism"—which is the state in which a believer lives as if he or she doesn't believe.

Both apatheism and practical atheism look the same at first glance—ignoring God. But after closer inspection you'll notice a fundamental difference between the two. Practical atheism is as old as the Old Testament. The psalmist complained about "foolish people" who believed in God but acted as if he didn't exist (Pss 14:1; 53:1). Thus, they were *practical* atheists, not actual atheists.

Today, these are the folks who attend church, zone out during the sermon, and live as if God doesn't matter to their lives. There is a profound disconnect between what they *believe* and how they *behave*. Scripture says that such practical atheists intentionally suppress their belief in God so that they can indulge in immorality. They don't find God questions irrelevant, neither do they reject God's existence. Instead, they reject his authority to speak into their lives as the standard of morality and goodness. So they act as if God doesn't exist. Apatheists, though, don't care at all about God, and this indifference causes them to act as if he doesn't exist.

It's subtle, but we must discern the difference. Otherwise, we risk issuing the wrong diagnosis. Approaching a practical atheist is, in some ways, more straightforward than approaching an apatheist. Practical atheists believe in God. They need reminding of what his existence means. Apatheists, however, don't care; they need to be convinced that his existence matters.

It's also important to consider that exhibiting apathy doesn't make a person an apatheist. Sometimes apathy is an indication of a serious mental and spiritual problem. It's not that people are merely apathetic toward God—they can't feel anything at all. God is caught up in their apathy toward life in general as they battle anxiety, depression, and emotional numbness. The apathy you witness isn't directed at God but is an absence of vitality, a loss of interest in everything. A persistent feeling of anxiety or perpetual fear arrests them and robs them of vitality. Even if they wanted to care about God, they couldn't. Sadness holds them captive while life slips by. They feel judged, powerless, and confused. They are numb, but, at the same time, everything hurts. These people need the kind of help that will navigate them through depression, like pastoral and licensed counselors can offer. Be sure not to confuse apatheism with an issue related to mental health.

Evangelizing the Apatheistic

Evangelizing the apatheistic is challenging for a few reasons. First, an apathetic heart toward God prevents people from experiencing the fullness of love. Apatheism runs contrary to everything in our understanding of the Creator and his creation. We are created in the image of God, who loves and is loved. In his triune being, the persons of God love one another: the Father loves the Son, the Son loves the Father, the Father and Son love the Spirit, and the Spirit loves the Father and the Son.

God has enjoyed love, both by giving and receiving affection, from eternity past and will continue to enjoy affection forever. Even before God created anything at all with the capacity to love and be loved—and even if God's creation ceased to be—he would still enjoy loving and being loved. God didn't create us so that he would have a way to love and to be loved, nor did God create love itself. No, God *is himself* love (1 John 4:8, 16).

God created us in his love-image out of divine, perfect affection so that we could enjoy the love that he is and enjoys. This love moved God to create and redeem us "to be holy and blameless in love before him" (Eph 1:4). This love mobilized the Lord Jesus from his heavenly throne to a bloody cross, "so that everyone who believes in him will not perish but have eternal life" (John 3:16). The power of this love moved God to pull Christ up from the tomb by the merit of his righteousness.

God's love is everlasting, a power so strong that it holds us as near and tightly to God's heart as his own Son. By faith in Christ, believers are hidden in him, incapable of being separated from the love of God, so that "the one who remains in love remains in God, and God remains in him" (Rom 8:37–39; 1 John 4:16). At its core, apatheism is not merely disinterest in the person of God but also in his love and good actions toward us. It is a holistic dismissal of God without consideration of who he is and what he does.

Second, because apatheism is altogether indifferent to God, it prevents apatheists from considering God questions. If you are a believer, apatheism leaves you puzzled. How can someone *not* care about the implications of God questions? This is bad news to more people than you'd think. Even atheists have good reason to be uncomfortable with that level of disinterest. It's far more advantageous for skeptics if the "Nones" were filled with atheists, not apatheists. If their goal is to eradicate belief, then apatheism is a known unknown. Maybe belief is still lurking below the surface of apathy, but, then again, perhaps it's not. It's better for skepticism if folks decide and declare that God doesn't exist rather than dismiss the question altogether.

Fellow religionists, like the Muslim I met in Cambridge, are puzzled too. Regardless of what they believe about God, at least other religions acknowledge the transcendent. In the end though, the apatheist's dismissal of God robs us all of the minimally common interest to discuss God questions. We are left standing in a vacant Areopagus with no one to hear our case for the gospel or other religious ideas. It seems impossible to start and sustain a conversation about God without it being terminated by disinterest, undermined by secularism, muted by comfort, or derailed by distraction.

Third, apatheism subverts an apatheist's ability to imagine a life of true and lasting fullness. If God is the core answer to our questions of origin, meaning, and joy, but we don't care at all about him, then we completely discount the primary reason that we "live and move and have our being" (Acts 17:28). We don't care that we are not our own, but that God owns us.

We were created by him, to live with him, for him, and to enjoy him forever. Apatheism is a devastating blow to pursuing fullness, especially as it relates to our joy, as we'll see in the next section.

So, how do we approach our neighbors in a way that overcomes their apathy for the sake of the gospel? This is the question I address in the second part of this book.

A good approach begins with self-reflection, an honest evaluation of how we imagine a life of fullness. In particular, it requires us to know our source of joy. We must understand our affections, whether or not our minds and hearts are stirred by God. Before ever striking up a conversation, we must first look ourselves in the mirror to address any apathy within. If our own hearts and minds are dulled toward God, what hope is a listless witness?

Only after we've put our own houses in order can we engage apatheism, remembering that it affects both mind and heart, so our approach must be big enough to capture both. We must take captive the thoughts and beliefs in opposition to the truth (2 Cor 10:5) by offering good reasons to care about God, but this is only half the task. We must also turn apathetic hearts joyward, that is, to the source of pure and lasting love. This is best done by modeling, in radical transparency, how God and his gospel bring us true and permanent joy.

But, before we attempt to enliven apatheists' hearts to our Creator and Redeemer, some other hearts need to be checked. And these hearts are as close to us as our own chests.

PART 2 | ENGAGING APATHEISM

"I've got the joy, joy, joy, joy down in my heart," I sang halfheartedly.

"Where?" the Sunday school teacher asked.

"Down in my heart," I said, staring at the carpet.

She asked again about the location of my joy.

"Down in my heart," I answered, just above a whisper.

Few things are more ironic than listlessly singing about joy. It's supposed to enliven us, to animate us with a sustained hope for something better and more than we experience in the present. Years ago, in my Sunday school classroom, I couldn't sing about joy because I didn't know joy's eternal source. I didn't understand who God was, what he did for me, and what he promised for me. So there I stood, with a finger up my nose, staring blankly at the floor. I didn't care, nor did I want to be at church if it weren't already obvious.

If I'm honest, some part of that kid still lives in me today. Even as a pastor, I find myself sometimes going through the motions. Not just during worship but also at home with my family, in the church with the flock I shepherd, and in the community, among the people I'm supposed to be evangelizing. I know God—my faith is in his promises; I confess his Son as Lord, and I know his Spirit dwells within me. But, admittedly, the joy that should come with knowing and being known by God sometimes evades me. The same reasons that lead apatheists to indifference, like comfort and distraction, lead me to an apathy that is indistinguishable from practical atheism.

I've given over to apathy more often than I'd care to admit, and I'm sure you have, too. Apathy zaps us of the joy of the Lord, which, among many bad things, undermines our evangelism. Let's call this what it is— sin. Apathy in believers transforms us into older versions of the young me listlessly singing "Joy, Joy Down in My Heart." We sing the right lyrics, articulate all the right theological and biblical positions, but our attitudes don't match the glory of the truths we communicate. We can talk all day long about how God created and sustains us, that he is good, faithful, and able to love us sinners. We can explain how he pardons our sins through the greatest sacrifice of love, the death of his Son, and that by faith in his life, death, and resurrection, we are liberated from the penalty and power of sin. We can describe how the Holy Spirit indwells us to reshape us in a mold of virtue, righteousness, and holiness. We can explain that God has vowed to resurrect us into a perfect, forever life, so that we live in a state of hopeful expectation sustained by confidence in God's promise for deliverance at Christ's future return.

But how effective is our witness if we share the gospel as if we're describing IRS tax code? If we aren't *underlining* the gospel with joy, aren't we *undermining* it? Doesn't the *way* we share the gospel communicate something about it? After all, if these things we believe are true, we should be filled with an unconquerable, imperishable joy. That joy should permeate all aspects of our lives, even amid sorrow, grief, and suffering (John 16:22). So, shouldn't joy fuel our evangelism, *showing* apatheists that God is far from irrelevant, instead of us just telling them so?

Joy certainly fueled the life of Christ and the early church. Some two thousand years ago, an angel appeared to Mary, declaring that her child would bring great joy for all people (Luke 2:10). Jesus taught that heaven erupts in joy when sinners repent (Luke 15:1–10). He looked forward to the cross in joy, "despising the shame," on his faithful march through death to his throne (Rom 8:34; Heb 12:2). Then, after his resurrection, in fear and great joy, some disciples ran from the empty tomb to tell the other disciples that Jesus had risen (Matt 28:8). After the Lord's ascension to heaven, the disciples returned to Jerusalem with great joy (Luke 24:52).

They were filled with joy and the Holy Spirit (Acts 13:52), for joy is the fruit found in him (Gal 5:22). In joy, the earliest Christians endured persecution (James 1:2) because they viewed their hardship as sharing in the suffering of Christ (1 Pet 4:13). The apostles, in turn, increased in joy as they heard reports of Christians growing in faithfulness (2 Cor 2:3; Phil 4:1; 1 Thess 2:19–20; Phlm 1:7; 3 John 1:4).

The kingdom of God expanded through the joy-filled lives of Christians, and today is no different. Joy ought to season our lives and propel us to the lost. Of all the apologetic arguments we can make, none are better than the life of a joy-filled believer. Faith in action, ignited by joy, is a credible display of the gospel. The way we live says a lot about what we believe and how we feel about those beliefs. If the gospel is the message, then we are the medium. So, when it comes to evangelism, the medium must match the message.

Instead, all too often, we act like I did in Sunday school, staring listlessly at carpet fibers, mumbling about how joy is, supposedly, "down in my heart to stay." When we have a joyless witness in an apathetic culture, the impression we give is that our faith isn't all that important. Even before we've said "hello," we've reinforced our neighbors' suspicion that belief in God doesn't satisfy any more or less than anything they've already experienced. We unintentionally advise against pursuing God as the avenue toward fullness.

Chapter 4 | Recapturing a Joyful Witness

I love my wife. There are a lot of reasons why. I find her to be beautiful, inside and out. She pursues godliness in private and, in public, has made it her life's mission to bear witness to the Lord Jesus as a godly business-woman. And she's *really* good at it. She's kind, brave, patient, and humble. She's a hard worker, always putting her best foot forward as she works for the Lord, not people, in everything she does. She's an incredible encourager, beyond gracious, and a great mom. Again, I love my wife.

Imagine, for a moment, meeting me in person for the first time. None of what I just wrote would be apparent to you. Sure, you'd see a wedding ring on my hand, but that metal band can only tell you so much. How would you ever know that I love my wife?

I suspect there are two ways: first, by watching me with her and, second, by the way I speak about her. If you were to follow me around for a while, the great affection I have for her would be evident. She captures my attention in a crowd. I habitually text "My Beautiful Bride" (her name in my phone) funny memes and updates about my day. She frequently comes up in stories I tell and is a recurring character in my sermons. I communicate my affection for her naturally through the way I live. And, if you were to ask me about her, I'd tell you all the things I just wrote.

Compelling arguments for my wife's existence wouldn't convince you of my affection for her. Explaining in philosophical terms her most valuable attributes wouldn't persuade you that I love her. It would convince you that

I'm weird—and you wouldn't be wrong—but it certainly wouldn't communicate my love for her.

I'm sure you know where I'm going with this. If we genuinely want apatheists to share our love for the Lord, then shouldn't our public witness begin with our affection for him? Brennan Manning bemoaned how often Christians bear witness to something they've not truly experienced, or, at the very least, it seems as if they have not. We act like "unconvicted and unpersuasive travel agents handing out brochures to places we have never visited."[1]

Apatheists don't need a compelling argument for God's existence, at least not at first. Remember, they don't care about God questions anyhow. What they need first is a convincing example of God's activity in our lives. Apatheists need travel agents who are happy to tell them about the place being advertised because they've been there and loved it. Apatheists need a credible witness of God's person and work. If apathy is the opposite of affection, and a faithful affection is where we want to help apatheists go, then we need first to show them what they're missing out on.

To clarify, I'm *not* arguing for an artificial happiness. It's easy to tell if someone's joy is genuine or synthetic. Trying to force joy in your witness will end up undermining you. It will communicate that Christianity doesn't have true joy, so Christians must hide behind a mask of blissful cheer.

Authentic joy is impossible to confuse with artificial happiness. It doesn't matter who you are or what your personality is like; joy in the heart is obvious. It's hard to fake delight. Regardless of where you land on the Enneagram, whether you are naturally chipper or shy, an introvert or an extrovert, joy shines through personality. Joy is a universal gift from the Holy Spirit that is meant to bless us, glorify God, and mark us Christians as his own. We need *that* kind of joy in our witness because it is to the source of joy itself that we invite the apathetic to find rest and fulfillment.

But we believers often run into a major problem. We look for happiness and joy in fallen, created things rather than in the holy Creator. So we need

---

[1] Brennan Manning, *The Ragamuffin Gospel* (Colorado Springs: Multnomah, 2005), 31.

a sanctified vision of fullness, which starts by repenting from looking for happiness and joy in anything but God first.

Searching for Happiness in All the Wrong Places

Don't you want to be happy?

It's a question we're often asked. Friends and family ask it when they express concern about our life choices, whether it's a stressful job or a troubled relationship. Advertisers implicitly ask it of us when they show us the happiness of others on vacation at a tropical resort or barreling down city streets in a sleek sports car.

All the best movies and television shows are about finding happiness. *The Office* followed the happiness that Jim Halpert and Pam Beasley found in each other. *The Shawshank Redemption* is a story about finding happiness in hope and freedom. *Good Will Hunting* directs us to look for happiness within ourselves. Everyone wants happiness.

Augustine pointed this out long ago. He asked, "Is not the happy life that which all desire, which indeed no one fails to desire?"[2] The answer, of course, is that all people, without exception, want to be happy, for "it is characteristic of all men to will to be happy."[3] It's why we get up in the morning, why we invest in relationships, and how we choose when and where to play. We want to have a happy life, to have joy. Our visions of fullness are interwoven with happiness.

And with good reason—we were created to enjoy happiness. Had our first parents not sinned, we would know lives filled with the peace and love that comes from perfect community with our Creator and each other. What other response than happiness is appropriate to that kind of life?

But our parents sinned, allowing sorrow to invade God's happy creation. Instead of finding happiness in the Creator, we began looking for it

---

[2] Augustine, *Confessions*, trans. Henry Chadwick (Oxford: Oxford University Press, 2008), 196.

[3] Augustine, *On The Trinity, Books 8–15*, 133.

in created things. And, instead of finding happiness in deeply meaningful relationships, we hid behind fig leaves. Now, happiness eludes us. It has degraded into the fleeting euphoria that comes with fun. Just as quickly as that kind of happiness arrives, it disappears. We settle for the temporary happiness in the feelings we get from earthly pleasure and play, but what we need is a return to the happiness grounded in heavenly joy. As C. S. Lewis reminded us, "Joy is the serious business of heaven."[4]

The change we need begins with reimagining happiness and joy primarily as something that *has us* rather than things *to be had*. We tend to think of happiness and joy as possessions. How often do people yearn to *have* joy and pleasure—to *have* a good time or to *have* a happy marriage? Happiness is something to pursue, to find, to earn, to keep and safeguard. Once we have happiness, we are afraid of losing it, as if it were a set of car keys. If you misplace happiness, you'll lose the ability to drive to the places you like the most.

Biblical happiness, on the other hand, is not primarily something we have. It is a joy that *has us*. Joy possesses us until it overtakes our whole lives. As Lewis said, "All Joy reminds. It is never a possession, always a desire for something longer ago or further away or still 'about to be.'"[5] The core of Christian happiness is the faith that reminds us of Christ, hopes for Christ, and anticipates Christ. Augustine said, "it is characteristic of all men to will to be happy, but," he clarified, "the faith, by which the heart is purified and arrives at happiness, is not characteristic of all."[6] Jonathan Edwards put it more explicitly: "[Christ] knew that all mankind were in the pursuit of happiness, he has directed them in the

---

[4] C. S. Lewis, *Letters to Malcolm: Chiefly on Prayer* (New York: Harvest Books, 1992), 93.

[5] C. S. Lewis, *Surprised By Joy: The Shape of My Early Life* (New York: HarperCollins, 2017), 93.

[6] Augustine, *On The Trinity*, 133.

true way to it, and he tells them what they must become in order to be blessed and happy."[7]

We all want joy, but not all of us have joy because not all of us have the faith to be had by Joy. Yes, I mean capital-J Joy, as in the eternal source of happiness, the true and living God himself. The Lord is our greatest source of joy because he is himself Joy (Ps 43:4).

This Joy is with us even when we are not having a good time. Joy grips us from rebirth to resurrection, and it never lets us go. It permeates all conditions of life, both good and bad times, because Joy is inseparable from the gospel and the Holy Spirit, who indwells believers. So Joy is with us when we are happy and Joy is with us when we are sad.

That's the difference in finding happiness in the holy Creator rather than the fallen creation. Happiness in this world is fickle. It's conditioned on circumstance. If you're having a good time, then you're happy. If you're not having a good time, then happiness eludes you. Biblical happiness, however, is constant because it's rooted in the consistency of our never-ending, unchanging God. It's not conditioned on circumstances. We can rejoice at weddings and funerals, at amusement parks and hospital beds, in coffee shops and courtrooms. Regardless of whether you are happy or sad, joy remains within a believer because God remains.

Moreover, happiness found in God is not the feeling we get from pleasure or play because it isn't something we can produce. Joy is a gift of God. It is the fruit of the Spirit (Gal 5:22). Joy is poured into our souls through the gospel, Scripture, and prayer. So the Christian life is not spent trying to be *happy*; rather, the Spirit indwells us to be made *holy* and filled with *joy*. We all want earthly happiness, but what we *need* is heavenly joy.

Again, it's not as though God does not want us to be happy. He does want happiness for us. But true happiness is a treasure buried deep in the holiness and glory of God. The heart that digs for joy in God is rich in

---

[7] Jonathan Edwards, *The Works of Jonathan Edwards*, vol. 2 (Edinburgh: Banner of Truth, 1974), 905.

happiness. You see, the problem isn't so much a pursuit of happiness *per se*. It isn't wrong to pursue happiness in the Creator. In fact, pursuing happiness in the Lord is a form of worship. John Piper's famous refrain is appropriate here: "God is most glorified in us when we are most satisfied in Him."[8] But so often, our pursuit of happiness is in the creation, rooted in idolatry.

Even though pure joy can only be found in God, we try very hard to find it elsewhere. Augustine's prayer captures this well: "You have made us for yourself, and our heart is restless until it comes to rest in you."[9] Our restless hearts flit from one source of happiness to another, always looking for the joy our souls crave, always seeking fullness. But most never find it because we're looking for the wrong thing in all the wrong places. We're looking for happiness in created things when we should be looking for joy in the Creator.

Finding Happiness in the Creation or Its Creator

What brings people happiness? The typical list of answers looks something like this: relationships, play, sex, money, careers, status, ideologies, causes, charities, exercise, entertainment, self-realization, etc. All of these things belong to the created order. They exist *within* and as *a part of* creation, all falling into one of three categories: (1) the self, (2) other people, and (3) things (See fig. 4.1).

It's probably most apparent to us that we look for happiness in other people. This is the reason we befriend, date, and marry. It's why we join communities and clubs and hang out at bars. It's why we spend hours on social media and dating apps. We yearn for relationships and community. We were designed for them, after all (Gen 2:18). We want friendships that make happy memories. We all want to find our "soul mates" to live *happily* ever after. We want families in which we feel safe and loved.

---

[8] John Piper, *Desiring God* (Sisters, OR: Multnomah, 2003), 288.

[9] Augustine, *Confessions*, trans. Thomas Williams (Indianapolis: Hackett, 2019), 1.

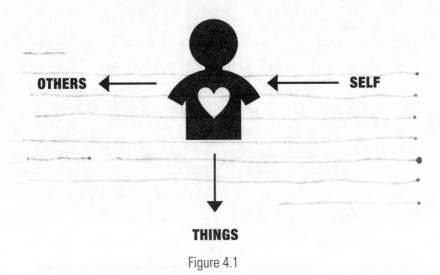

THINGS

Figure 4.1

We also look for happiness in things, anything from toys and hobbies to work and wealth. We train our hearts to embrace material objects and immaterial ideas or statuses. We promise ourselves that if we can only reach a higher level, then we will be truly happy. If we can only graduate college, get promoted, and achieve a certain amount of income, then we will have happiness. Ideas and causes, too, are things in which we participate to find happiness. Perhaps happiness is located in the right state of mind, so we search for the right philosophy. Or maybe happiness is found in bringing justice to the world, so we put our energy into politics.

We also look for happiness in ourselves. We're told that happiness can be found by genuinely knowing and accepting oneself, so we turn to meditation and inward reflection. The better we understand ourselves, we're told, the more we can appreciate ourselves. And there, tucked deep within self-realization, is a rich vein of happiness we can mine.

Do these things make us happy? Not in the long run. Yet this is the lie we believe: if you want to be happy, look within and around you because real joy is found in creation.

This is an empty promise, and believing this lie prevents people from understanding the truth. Not understanding truth prevents us from experiencing joy. It's a vicious cycle. Augustine asked, "How shall the soul rejoice in truth, whose joy is founded on falsehood?"[10] It can't. True joy is found in the Creator, not his creation. And lasting happiness is found in God, not what he has made. For, as Paul says, "The kingdom of God is not eating and drinking, but righteousness, peace, and joy in the Holy Spirit" (Rom 14:17). So, pray with Augustine: "The happy life, in fact, is joy in truth: and that means joy in you, who are Truth, O God."[11] We must train our hearts to love him above all else, to look heavenward for joy, not around us for happiness (See fig. 4.2). "To rejoice for you, in you, about you: this is itself the happy life, this alone, and no other," said Augustine.[12]

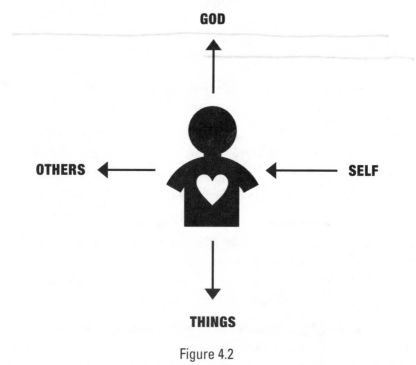

Figure 4.2

---

[10] Augustine, *City of God*, trans. Marcus Dods (New York: Modern Library, 1993), 339.

[11] Augustine, *Confessions*, 181.

[12] Augustine, 181.

God is not the cosmic killjoy that he is so often portrayed. In fact, the fleeting happiness we find in creation is a reflection of the joy we find in God because created things are gifts from him. Your spouse, your family, your friends—all gifts from God. And you—yes, *you*—are a gift to others. These gifts give us glimpses of God; they are reflections of his goodness. It's not the objects themselves that bring joy; instead, it is through them that we experience a foretaste of Joy. Our lives as believers are rehearsals for living with Joy forever. The joy of your wedding day, the joy of hearing your child laugh for the first time, the joy of embracing old friends: We are happy in those moments, and rightly so. But such momentary happiness is meant to remind us of a greater joy still to come.

When we lose that perspective, or if we never gain it, we demand from gifts what only the gift-giver can offer. What happens, then, when we are *unhappy* with our gifts? What happens when we argue with our spouses, when our children disobey, or when friends become enemies? What happens when we get passed over for promotion or an economic dip wipes away our wealth? What happens when, after years of meditation, we still aren't happy?

Let me ask more probing questions. What do we do when confronted with sin and death? What happens when loved ones are taken from us? What happens when good relationships turn harmful, when we are robbed, oppressed, or violated? What happens when the only thing self-realization brings is unsettling darkness from within?

We are sad in those moments, and rightly so. The momentary sadness makes us realize that earthly happiness is fleeting. It gently reminds our souls that we were meant for more than mere happiness in created things. We were meant for eternal joy, a happiness that is both sustained and sustaining through sorrow because its source is God. It is unmoved by circumstance, so it carries us along through grief. This deep and abiding joy is a hallmark of the Christian faith. Looking backward through the cross, we believers look forward to a new creation and rejoice.

Chapter 5 | The Paradox of Joy

The Christian faith audaciously declares that joy and sorrow coexist. If that sounds like a paradox, it is. How can joy and suffering live side by side? When you think about it, joy as a hallmark of Christianity seems contradictory. It comes across as naive, as if faith makes one ignorant of all the sorrow in the world. Barely a day goes by when we are not faced with suffering and heartache. We are keenly aware that people all over the world suffer, whether it's from tyrannical governments, failed economies, disease, violence, injustice, oppression, wars, or natural disasters. And the story of the gospel itself initially seems to culminate in the unjust murder of Christ! How, then, can Christianity promote joy, especially when its most recognized symbol is a cross?

Yet there it is. Joy and misery stand side by side. The shape of the cross itself represents the intersection of joy and sorrow, pain and glory, all meeting in the dying body of the Lord Jesus. Indeed, it was for the *joy* laid before Jesus that he endured the cross (Heb 12:2). Christ alone offers us the happiness of life through the sorrow of death. Through the Comforter's power, God's affection for his people lifts their chins upward in valleys of darkness. "Let me hear joy and gladness," prays the psalmist, "let the bones you have crushed rejoice" (Ps 51:8). Why? Because joy transcends circumstance. Tucked deep within joy is its key ingredient—hope. It causes us to look backward in remembrance of God's goodness and forward in anticipation of his faithfulness. Christian joy isn't a contradiction;

it's an invitation, a promise that our Redeemer has caused his people to sing about how "joy and gladness will overtake them, and sorrow and sighing will flee" (Isa 35:10).

True, the universal symbol of Christianity is a cross, but Jesus didn't remain on it. He rose again, promising a spectacular return that will forever upend sin and sorrow. We live in a whole new world now, one in which God's peace—his eternal *shalom*—is storming the gates of Hades and invading the enemy's kingdom, liberating the oppressed and bringing true justice as hearts submit to Jesus as Lord. No ideology or politic can do what Jesus will (and has already begun to) accomplish.

That's where we believers find our joy—in the death *and* resurrection of the Lord Jesus. His death paid for our sins, and his resurrection proved the sufficiency of his sacrifice, earning him authority over all things. Now, by faith, we are given new life and new citizenship in a whole new world, one ruled by King Jesus, who has promised to come down from heaven and resurrect us forever from all brokenness at his return.

So, "our citizenship is in heaven, and we eagerly wait for a Savior from there, the Lord Jesus Christ. He will transform the body of our humble condition into the likeness of his glorious body, by the power that enables him to subject everything to himself" (Phil 3:20–21). This promise never fades; it never weakens. It is powerful and permanent. It is never subject to how things are getting on in the world. This promise of resurrection and rescue is as genuine and inevitable as God himself.

Ours is a joy that comes by the goodness and faithfulness of God. And because God is never-ending and consistent, regardless of circumstances, so is our joy. Even in the worst of times, when joy seems inappropriate or unwarranted, we Christians can rejoice.

Joy Because Of and Joy In Spite Of

The Bible teaches us that all joy comes as a result of God and despite circumstances. Joy is two-fold from one source; joy is *found* in God and *sustained* by God. Augustine noticed this when he defined the happy life as one in which joy is "grounded in [God] and caused by [God]."[1] Biblical scholars, too, have noticed how Christian joy is twofold, a (1) joy *because of* and (2) joy *in spite of*.[2] We rejoice *because of* God and his redemptive action, and we rejoice *in spite of* circumstances that bring grief and sorrow.

Take, for example, Habakkuk's response to an impending invasion by Babylonian forces. Habakkuk's soul trembled at the prospect of war. He cried,

> I heard, and I trembled within; my lips quivered at the sound.
> Rottenness entered my bones; I trembled where I stood.
> Now I must quietly wait for the day of distress
> to come against the people invading us. (Hab 3:16)

To make matters worse, it seemed like the whole countryside had collapsed in anxiety-causing problems. Habakkuk continued,

> Though the fig tree does not bud and there is no fruit on the vines,
> though the olive crop fails and the fields produce no food,
> though the flocks disappear from the pen and there are no herds in
> the stalls. . . . (Hab 3:17)

By all accounts, Habakkuk had nothing to be happy about. War was coming, and famine accompanied it. Death and suffering were on the horizon. Nevertheless, Habakkuk declared, "Yet I will celebrate in the LORD; I will *rejoice* in the God of my salvation" (Hab 3:18).

---

[1] Augustine, *Confessions*, trans. Henry Chadwick, 412 (see chap. 4, n. 2).

[2] See Miroslav Volf and Justin E. Crisp, eds., *Joy and Human Flourishing: Essays on Theology, Culture, and the Good Life*, eds. Miroslav Volf and Justin Crisp (Minneapolis, MN: Fortress Press, 2015). In "Reflections on Joy in the Bible" (pp. 17–38), Marianne Meye Thompson noticed this pattern, classifying the rejoicing as "joy because of " and "joy notwithstanding." In the same work, in his essay "Joy: Some New Testament Perspectives and Question" (pp. 39–62), N. T. Wright similarly notes that there is a *reason* for joy and a specific *character* of joy.

How can that possibly be? What had he to rejoice in? He told us: "The LORD my Lord is my strength; he makes my feet like those of a deer and enables me to walk on mountain heights!" (Hab 3:19).

Habakkuk had joy *because of* God's salvation and *in spite of* impending war and famine. In the same way, we as Christians have joy *because of* what God has done through the Lord Jesus Christ, and we rejoice *in spite of* our circumstances, whether we are healthy or hurting, satisfied or suffering, glad or grieved. With Christ, it's possible to smile amid poverty, to rejoice in the face of cancer, and laugh through tears. After all, we know that one day soon death will die, all our tears will be wiped away, and our evening strolls will be on streets of gold (Rev 20:14; 21:4, 21).

This is joy: by grace alone, we believers have experienced the goodness and faithfulness of God in the death and resurrection of his Son, and that, in faith, the Holy Spirit fills us with confidence in the goodness and faithfulness of God yet to come. As Jonathan Edwards said, "Christ purchased for us spiritual joy and comfort, which is in a participation of God's joy and happiness; which joy and happiness is the Holy Ghost."[3] So, in good conscience and with good reason, we Christians can sing "It is well with my soul" during good times when "peace like a river attendeth my way" *and* during bad times when "sorrows like sea billows roll."[4]

The real contradiction, then, isn't joyful Christianity but apathetic Christianity. To be Christian—to be delivered from death to life by God, in and through the Lord Jesus, filled with the Holy Spirit—is to be someone who experiences joy regardless of life circumstances. Marianne Thompson's thought is helpful: "Because joy is grounded in the expectation of God's deliverance, it has the character of perseverance, confidence, and trust [and] cannot be disturbed by external circumstances."[5]

---

[3] Jonathan Edwards, *The Works of Jonathan Edwards*, vol. 21, ed. Sang Hyun Lee (New Haven, CT: Yale University Press, 2003), 136.

[4] Horatio Spafford, "It Is Well with My Soul," 1878.

[5] Marianne Meye Thompson, "Reflections on Joy in the Bible," in Volf and Crisp, *Joy and Human Flourishing*, 37.

Paul referenced this joy when he commanded the Philippians to "rejoice in the Lord *always*" (Phil 4:4). By always, he meant *always*. There is no asterisk in the Greek, to warn that certain exclusions may apply.

At face value, his advice seems impossible, even a bit crass. But Paul is not writing from an ivory tower. In the same letter, he demonstrates how his joy sustained him during his lowest points. He experienced imprisonment (Phil 1:7, 14), rivalry (1:15–17), suffering (1:29–30), sorrow (2:27), anxiety (2:28), lowness, hunger, need (4:12), and troubles (4:14). And we know from Scripture that he experienced beatings, stoning, illness, and even shipwreck. Yet, in all these things, he found the secret of abiding in joy, the Lord God; he remembered that the secret to joy had found him (Phil 4:13; Acts 9:1–5). Paul bids us to follow his example in rejoicing always, no matter what.

But, unless I'm alone in this, don't we still find ourselves in bouts of joyless apathy from time to time? It's as if we hear Paul saying, "You *better* rejoice or else!" As if the apostle isn't inviting us into a blessing of joy. So, we respond to his command with a snippy and sulky, "Ha, easier said than done"? Are you like me? If so, we need to address this problem before evangelizing apatheists. We need to recapture joy in our witness, to hear Paul giving us an invitation more than a demand to rejoice always. To do so, we need to understand what causes joyless faith. How is it that Christians can lose their affection for God, finding no real joy in him at all? I think, in large part, the answer has to do with spiritual amnesia. We forget who we are and whose we are. When we do, we fall short. Only repentance and grace can lift us up again.

Spiritual Amnesia and Idolatry

It doesn't seem possible for a believer to forget God, but it happens. A lot. We live in the same comfortable, distracted society as our apathetic neighbors. We naively assume that our daily bread comes from restaurants, our healing from hospitals, and our rest from entertainment. The Holy Spirit is our Comforter only when we want him to be. We page him when we are troubled by serious issues like grief or depression. Until then, we're comforted by our comfortable society.

And every day, like our unbelieving neighbors, we face the same torrent of information and tasks that divide our limited attention among a million separate issues. I'm willing to bet for most of us, the first thing we do in the morning involves social media and calendars, not prayer and Scripture reading; workflows, not worship. In short, the same reasons that move our neighbors to apathy cause amnesia in us. We only care about God when we remember he's there.

We also have a bad habit of forgetting who we are. Fundamentally, humans are God's image bearers, a unique creation "according to his likeness," designed for community with him, and cared for by him (Gen 1:26–27; Ps 8:4). Even as Christians, we are sinners, of course, but that is not original to our design. To be a sinner is not human nature but *fallen* human nature. Our human nature has been pervasivly tainted by sin, but to be truly human means to be truly God's in body, mind, and soul. And once we trust in Christ, we are God's "workmanship, created in Christ Jesus for good works, which God prepared ahead of time for us to do" (Eph 2:10). God made us for himself, and he is ultimately good, faithful, and able. His great promise for us, his redeemed children, involves taking delight in him forever (Rev 7:9–10).

The Westminster Shorter Catechism captures the wisdom of Scripture on humanity like this: "Man's chief end is to glorify God, and to enjoy him forever." But even Christians often forget this truth. When temptation sets in and mistrust of God builds, we are quick to recast ourselves as someone we're not meant to be—people who search for joy in creation, not the Creator. We upend the catechism to say, "Man's chief end is to glorify creation, and take misery in it forever."

Is God the greatest source of joy in your life? He must be. We were created to "enjoy him forever," and Christians will! As Piper put it, "Happiness in God is the end of all our seeking. Nothing beyond it can be sought as a higher goal."[6] Nothing brings us fullness, the authentic and enduring joy for which we yearn, like knowing, loving, and walking with God. We

---

[6] Piper, *Desiring God*, 60 (see chap. 4, n. 8).

try, though. We look to creation to bring us happiness, splitting our hearts between heaven and earth. But finding the ultimate source of our joy in anything other than God is idolatry, which is to demand from something created that which only the Creator can give. Rather than saying "In *him* we live and move and have our being," we say "In *it* we live and move and have our being" (Acts 17:28). Again, we ask of the gifts what only the gift giver can offer. We reject God's offer for a joyful life and pursue what brings us only temporary happiness, even if that happiness stretches over long periods.

Now we're orbiting the root cause of apathy toward God—*idolatry*. It's more than bowing before stone statues. Idolatry is worshiping anything or anyone other than the One who deserves our adoration. We look for meaning and purpose and joy according to our terms and in places we select. Sure, idolatry can involve effigies, but it's more pervasive than that. We worship our stuff, careers, money, and relationships. We sacrifice time and treasure in exchange for happiness. But how often have they disappointed? How often have our idols failed us, betrayed us, or fallen apart before us? We ask our idols for true and lasting joy, but they give us empty and momentary happiness instead. It's not as though Paul found tent making meaningless. I have no doubt that he relished in being known as a quality tentmaker. But, when the economy grew sluggish and demand for tents evaporated, Paul knew his life still had meaning.

All idols are temporary, shallow, dull, and hollow. They give us happiness for a season but inevitably fail to sustain our joy. They are the first to break during times of grief and suffering. They are quick to betray us when another more valued worshiper appears before them. Worst of all, idolatry is a rejection of the living God, of all that is good, faithful, and true. Yet we keep coming back to idols. And the longer we worship them, the more like them we become.

Gregory Beale noticed this pattern in Scripture. He observed that "what people revere, they resemble, either for ruin or for restoration."[7] If we worship

---

[7] Gregory K. Beale, *We Become What We Worship: A Biblical Theology of Idolatry* (Downers Grove, IL: InterVarsity Press, 2008), 16.

an idol, we become like that idol. If we worship God, we become like him. Beale pointed to Ps 115:4–8 and Isa 6:9–10 as examples. In the psalm, idolaters are said to be "just like" their idols, immobile and unable to use their senses.

> Their idols are silver and gold, made by human hands.
> They have mouths but cannot speak, eyes, but cannot see.
> They have ears but cannot hear, noses, but cannot smell.
> They have hands but cannot feel, feet, but cannot walk.
> They cannot make a sound with their throats.
> Those who make them are *just like them*, as are all who trust in them (emphasis added).

The nations worshiped things they could see and feel; but Israel, of all peoples, knew better. The first two commandments God gave Israel forbade them to worship other gods and to craft idols. Yet we know the story—they habitually fell into idolatry anyhow. By Isaiah's day, the land was chock-full of idols. God lamented over his people: "They worship the work of their hands, what their fingers have made" (Isa 2:8). They were no different than the ignorant nations who were worshiping immobile, non-sensing figurines. As a result, the Israelites looked less like God and more like idols—deaf to God and blind to truth. It's no wonder, then, that God commissioned Isaiah to warn idolaters: "Go! Say to these people: Keep listening, but do not understand; keep looking, but do not perceive. Make the minds of these people dull; deafen their ears and blind their eyes" (Isa 6:9–10).

All idols are blind and deaf, as cold and lifeless as the material they are made from. They cannot see God nor hear the truth, and neither can they *feel* him. They have no affection toward him because they have no hearts. Idols are incapable of loving God. Is it any wonder, then, that we become like what we worship—deaf, blind, and apathetic to our eternal source of joy?

Repentance That Leads to Remembrance

Recapturing our joyful witness begins with repentance. We must confess our idolatry to God like David did: "Against you—you alone—I have sinned and done this evil in your sight" (Ps 51:4). And we must trust that God is good to respond to our plea, "Restore the joy of your salvation to me" (v. 12). He will, and he does. God rejoices at our repentance, embracing us like the returned prodigal sons and daughters we are. And the joy he experiences from wrapping his arms around our repentant souls flows into us. When we "relish the excellency of the divine nature," Edwards wrote, "[we] will incline to be with him and to enjoy him."[8]

We should also be people who are in the habit of reminding ourselves of God and praising him. Does it feel a bit sacrilegious to need reminding about God Almighty? Ideally, we'd never need to be reminded because God would be with us. We could walk with him in the cool of the day (see Gen 3:8). But we aren't in the garden any longer. We are east of Eden, where forgetfulness is a universal issue.

In the Old Testament, the people of God were commanded to recite a proclamation called the *Shema* twice a day (Deut 6:7). It was a declaration that reminded them about God and their relationship to him. "Listen, Israel: The LORD our God, the LORD is one. Love the LORD your God with all your heart, with all your soul, and with all your strength" (vv. 4–5). These words were meant to be in the heart of every Israelite, to be memorized, internalized, repeated, taught, and acted upon (vv. 6–9). They even wore tassels as a visual reminder that they were the people of God (Num 15:38–39). Given that Yahweh was so foundational to Israel's identity, you'd think they wouldn't need reminders, but they did. And so do we. If it was easy to forget God in ancient Israel, how much easier is it for us living in our secular, distracted, and comfortable society? There is so much conflict, so much to do, so much to enjoy, so much to oppose. Our attention span for God diminishes quickly in our restless living.

We as believers ought to develop worshipful habits that remind us, over and again, that God loves us, and our highest purpose is to enjoy him. We need a *Shema*, a constant nudging back to what matters most. I think this looks a little different for everyone, but practicing spiritual disciplines and

---

[8] Edwards, *Works of Jonathan Edwards*, ed. Sang Hyun Lee, 174.

living in Christian community are essential. Let them be our tassels, our reminders to look heavenward for our joy.

Yet, even with our tassels and habits, we are still absent-minded creatures prone to forget our Creator. We need help to remember. God knows this, which is why he sent us the Counselor, the Holy Spirit, who bears witness of Christ and brings all things to our remembrance (John 14:26). We must lean into the Spirit to remind us of redemption and salvation, the gospel in which we stand.

A Spirit-directed remembrance of God leads to worshiping him with all our hearts, souls, and strength. And to love God wholly, with everything we are, inevitably leads to joy. Only after we've recaptured our joyful witness can we approach apatheistic neighbors. Apatheists ought to be drawn to the gospel through our lives, being especially attracted to the joy we display no matter our state. Whether things are going well or poorly, in times of happiness and despair, there should be a joy so distinct and peculiar that it forces the apatheist to desire what we have been given.

So, as Christians, we ought to examine our hearts and minds to uncover and root out apathy. What good will it do for a practical atheist to try to convince an apatheist of the glory of God? This means reimagining faith as a fundamental change in our mode of living. Belief in God and trust in his promises are not merely ornaments and accessories to our worldview—they are fundamentals intended to change us completely. We ought to posture ourselves as living examples of how Christianity is not something to merely add to one's beliefs but is the rubric through which we accept or reject and understand all beliefs.

Chapter 6 | How We Share When They Don't Care

We began this book by asking how we might share the gospel with our apathetic neighbors. Before answering that question, we had a lot of ground to cover. We needed to know the conditions in which apatheism arises and to explore apatheism in detail. We also needed to consider how apathy toward God affects us. Now, it's time to put what we've learned into practice. Having recaptured our joyful witness, we turn our attention to approaching apatheism.

These are some key things to remember:

(1) Apatheism is a duality that affects both beliefs and feelings; that is, apatheists *believe* that God is unimportant and *feel* that way as well.

(2) Apatheism flourishes within certain cultural conditions in which belief in God is contested and diverse and people are comfortable and distracted.

(3) All people yearn for joy, for which God is the only true and lasting source.

(4) Apatheists don't care about the source of joy, but they desire it nonetheless.

For these reasons, our approach must . . .

(1) Speak to both mind and heart, challenging both beliefs and feelings about God.

(2) Take into account that no two apatheists are the same—they will likely display some combinativeness when approached with the gospel—so

no one-size-fits-all approach will work, and they must experience a disruption in their distracted, comfortable lives before the gospel can grasp them.

(3) Take into account the sources of joy each apatheist is pursuing.

(4) Proclaim through word and testimony that God is the true and lasting source of joy.

That last point is crucial. Apatheists won't care about God, but they will care about that which only God can give. They pursue joy—we all do. But they look in all the wrong places. They've exchanged joy for the happiness they find in themselves, others, and things. God isn't considered a source of joy because they lack the reason and motivation to consider him. Our goal, then, is to give them reasons and motivations to search for joy in God, which can only come by faith in the gospel.

But how is that possible for someone who doesn't care about God? How do we show someone the Way to joy when he is stuck in the snare of indifference?

Modifying Our Apologetic Approach

Certainly, we should reject bold, in-your-face evangelistic strategies. It's counterintuitive—even obnoxious and insincere—to argue aggressively with people for the desirability of Christian joy. Instead, our initial instinct should be to marry a winsome attitude with apologetics, the art of crafting and making arguments for the defense of Christian truth claims. Apologetics seeks to answer objections to the gospel in an engaging manner that makes the faith plausible and, hopefully, believable to unbelievers. If apatheists do not care about God, then perhaps we can zap them out of their indifference, not with aggression, but by amiably appealing to various apologetic approaches, e.g., classical approach, presuppositionalism, Reformed epistemology, evidentialism, and cumulative case.[1]

---

[1] For a helpful introduction to these methods, see Brian K. Morley, *Mapping Apologetics: Comparing Contemporary Approaches* (Downers Grove, IL: InterVarsity Press, 2015).

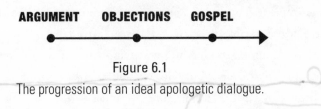

ARGUMENT   OBJECTIONS   GOSPEL

Figure 6.1

The progression of an ideal apologetic dialogue.

Yet I'm afraid that these methods may fall on deaf ears with apatheism. Consider how an apologist typically approaches a skeptic (see fig. 6.1). The conversation usually begins with the apologist offering persuasive arguments for the plausibility of God's existence by appealing to the skeptic's reason and conscience (e.g., cosmological, teleological, ontological, and moral arguments). The skeptic hears the argument, then responds positively or negatively. If the response is negative, the apologist does what she can to answer objections, sparring over the argument, but the conversation presses forward from mere theism to Christian theism. The goal, of course, is not to demonstrate the plausibility of just any transcendent being, but the existence of the God of Scripture, so the conversation draws to a close with the proclamation of the gospel. Lord willing, the conversation blossoms in a faith declaration and leads to discipleship in the future.

A conversation like this is only possible if both parties are actually interested in God questions. Naturally, the Christian apologist is interested in such questions. Very often, so are fellow religionists and engaged skeptics. Think back to my conversation with the Muslim in Cambridge. We shared a minimally common interest in God questions. But what about an apatheist? Unfortunately, there is no shared minimally common interest in God questions. Our Athens lacks a statue to the unknown god. An apatheist finds God and God questions irrelevant, uninteresting, and perhaps even undesirable. This is why apatheism is far more challenging for evangelism than religious pluralism, atheism, and agnosticism. Apathy robs us of the common interest in God that sparks the kind of gospel conversations we enjoy with skeptics and unbelievers.

What are we to do? Should we ditch apologetics altogether? No, of course not. It would be foolish to abandon something that is not only a biblical imperative (1 Pet 3:15) but also a tool actively used by the Holy Spirit to draw people to the Lord Jesus. Instead, we must modify—not jettison—our apologetic method when approaching apatheism because we start apologetic conversations with apatheists in a deficit of interest. Rather than beginning with God questions, we must perform a prefatory maneuver. We need to gain their interest in God questions before moving into familiar apologetic territory.

But, if they're not interested in God, where do we even begin?

Overcoming Apathy with Doubt

The nineteenth-century philosopher Søren Kierkegaard wrestled with apathy in his day. He was born into an affluent family in Copenhagen. Like other European nations, Denmark supported an official church. Kierkegaard lamented that his fellow citizens had become lulled into a false sense of identity living in Christendom. To be Danish was to be a Christian, or so they thought. For many people, faith was more about citizenship than relationship, which produced an apathy of spiritual faith. In effect, to Kierkegaard, Denmark became a nation of practical atheists. They didn't take their faith seriously at all. But he wanted to challenge their indifference. To be genuinely Christian was not to be a member of the state church; rather, it meant having an unconditional, individual commitment to the faith.

Like us, Kierkegaard recognized that having conversations about faith is difficult if your conversation partner is apathetic. Asking people to think critically about something they don't care about doesn't typically pan out. They don't want to think about it. The only way to overcome apathy is to compel someone to self-reflection that is sustained long enough to allow for critical thinking. But what could possibly compel someone past indifference to interest?

The answer, for Kierkegaard, is doubt. Not the kind of doubt we're used to in the Bible (i.e., mistrusting God), but an uncertainty that causes us to investigate our assumptions. He argued that "doubt is a higher form than any objective thinking, for it presupposes the latter but has something more, a third, which is interest."[2] In other words, doubt is a type of thinking that's more powerful than mere objective thought alone. We only think about something for an extended period of time when we're interested in it. The uncertainty that accompanies doubt throws interest into the mix. If our beliefs are built on assumptions, then doubt is a thought earthquake. It destabilizes us for a moment, forcing us to move. And, in that moment, we become curious. What caused the earthquake? What beliefs were damaged in the process? And what beliefs need to be strengthened to avoid damage in the future? Curiosity overtakes apathy, motivating us to discover and find answers. In short, doubt motivates us to think about things we didn't care about before.

This is why we shouldn't start conversations with apatheists by asking them to think objectively about God questions. Apathy drains those questions of their power. Instead, the first step we must prompt them to take is not upward to God but inward to the self (See fig. 6.2). To borrow Francis Schaeffer's language, we must first identify "points of tension" that exist in the lives of apatheists.[3] For Schaeffer, whoever holds non-Christian beliefs about the world strays from reality because only Christianity presents the world as it truly is. For this reason, unbelievers live with various tension points, conflicts between personal conviction and reality, as they live inconsistently in the world. Christianity isn't guilty of creating an imaginary world, as Karl Marx claimed. The opposite is true—non-Christian beliefs are the imaginary world builders.

DOUBT   ARGUMENT   OBJECTIONS   GOSPEL

Figure 6.2
Before God questions can be asked, apatheists must first doubt
their reasons and motivations for being indifferent to God.

---

[2] Søren Kierkegaard, *Johannes Climacus*, ed. and trans. Howard V. Hong and Edna H. Hong (Princeton: Princeton University Press, 1985), 170.

[3] Francis Schaeffer, *The God Who Is There*, in *Schaeffer Trilogy: Three Essential Books in One Volume* (Wheaton, IL: Crossway, 1990), 129–35.

Schaffer argued (somewhat anticipating Charles Taylor's "buffered self") that to shelter themselves from this conflict of belief and reality, each person has "built a roof over his head to shield himself at the point of tension."[4] The job of the apologist is to gently and lovingly push on these tension points to remove the roof. This approach exposes the "internal world" of the unbeliever to the "external world" (i.e., reality).[5] "When the roof is off," Schaffer said, "each man must stand naked and wounded before the truth of what is."[6] This roof removal produces the desired doubt. And if apatheists *doubt* their beliefs, then their doubt will stir within them curiosity-driven interest.

[4] Schaeffer, *God Who Is There*, 140.
[5] Schaeffer, 140.
[6] Schaeffer, 140.

Chapter 7 | Engaging Apatheism in Conversation

What, exactly, should apatheists doubt about their beliefs? What are the tension points to press to remove their roofs? The most effective encounters I've had are conversations that orbited our conceptions of fullness, especially as it relates to joy. For this reason, it has been my experience that "cultural apologetics" is the most effective approach at winning the attention of an apatheist. Cultural apologetics draws on cultural evidences (e.g., art, music, literature) and universal, existential human longings to argue for the truth and fullness of Christianity.[1] Instead of presenting Christian belief primarily as *reasonable*, as is the goal of other apologetic methods, cultural apologetics seeks to present Christian belief primarily as *desirable*. It is not as though the other methods do not present Christianity as desirable but the focus of those conversations is typically on the veracity of Christian belief. Likewise, cultural apologetics contends for the truthfulness of Christianity, but the weight of conversation leans into human longing and desires, especially as they are communicated in one's culture.

What does it mean to live a life of fullness? It means to know why we live, what meaning we hold, and what brings us the greatest joy. Questions about fullness and joy have yielded the most fruitful conversations I've had with apatheists. I want an honest evaluation of their joy and mine because

---

[1] For an excellent introduction to cultural apologetics, see Paul M. Gould, *Cultural Apologetics: Renewing the Christian Voice, Conscience, and Imagination in a Disenchanted World* (Grand Rapids: Zondervan, 2019).

joy is such an integral part of fulfillment. Specifically, I hope to challenge apatheists that their joy might not be as powerful and permanent as they think (a point of tension), and that the one thing they find irrelevant, belief in God, leads to a more powerful and permanent state of joy. The goal of these conversations is not conversion but consideration. I want them to doubt their sources of joy, to consider that they may be partial and fleeting whereas God as a source of joy is robust and enduring. I want them to consider the shortcomings of their sources of joy, to consider the importance of God, and to consider the gospel.

These aren't agenda-driven conversations; they're goal-oriented encounters. In agenda-driven conversations, there is an undue pressure to get the apatheist to care right then and there. As far as I've experienced, barring an intervention by the Holy Spirit, this is an impossible task. There's no way to shock apatheists out of their indifference with arguments and facts. If your agenda is to get them to care right away, then you'll be driven by a motivation that hinders the whole conversation. You'll ask questions like, "How can you not care about God?" or "Don't you realize how arrogant and dangerous it is to be indifferent to him?" This approach puts them on edge and only pushes them deeper into apathy. You don't need to bark at them about why indifference is bad; instead, you need to show them how belief is good.

This is why I prefer goal-oriented encounters. The goal, of course, is building interest in and consideration of God. It's a goal to strive toward, not a switch to flip on. In goal-oriented encounters, there is freedom to keep pace with apatheists, however quickly or slowly they move. We want them to hear the gospel without apathy getting in the way. We want them to reimagine the God they find to be irrelevant, whether it happens during the conversation or later on.

These conversations typically occur in three phases:

(1) First, I have them tell me what brings them the greatest amount of joy.

(2) Second, I ask them to consider the fragility and impermanence of their sources of joy, causing them to doubt those sources.

(3) Third, I describe how God is a powerful and permanent source
of joy through the gospel and my testimony.

Let's examine these one by one as I interweave a fictional (although based on
reality) conversation with an apatheist named Justin.

Before going forward, I feel the need to offer a caveat. It goes without
saying that what follows is merely an example based on my experiences.
My goal is not to prescribe the exact steps you must follow when sharing
with those who don't care. I want to offer up one practical method I've used
regarding how we might share when an opportunity is given.

Phase 1: What Brings Us the Greatest Joy in Life?

I'll start by asking Justin to tell me about what brings him the most joy in
life. I'm careful not to ask what brings him joy. The answer will be too short:
"my family," "my career," "my hobby." I want him to *tell* me about his joy
bringers, to narrate how those things bring him happiness. Very rarely does
only one thing bring joy, so I ask what else brings joy. There are no right or
wrong answers.

Importantly, I genuinely want to know what makes Justin happy.
Apatheists aren't my project; they're my fellow image bearers whom God
loves and wants for himself. So I want them to reveal their hearts, their
desires, their wants. This is the same thing Jesus did. One of his favorite
questions to ask people wasn't "what do you *think*?" nor "how do you *feel*?"
but "what do you *want*?" (Matt 20:21, 31; Mark 10:36, 51; Luke 18:41).
Wanting gets at both thinking and feeling. Asking about joy is asking about
a person's wants because desires reveal our sources of happiness.

The goal is to genuinely understand our neighbors. I want to talk about
what brings them joy. I want to know about the relationships that move
them, the books that stir them, the music they enjoy; but I also want to talk
about what happens if those joy bringers fail, thereby introducing doubt
that brings interest.

"Tell me about what brings you the greatest joy in life," I ask.

People are typically taken off guard by this request. It's not something we think about often, let alone expect to be asked about. Inevitably, the answer involves finding joy in other people, things and activities, or themselves. Usually, in that order, too. By far, the place where people find the most happiness is in relationships. They love their significant others, family, friends, and communities. From marriages to social clubs, relationships are typically our most significant source of joy.

Sometimes people will respond with things they have or things they do. They have an antique car or a favorite pastime, or they love their job. They count down the hours before they can hitch their bass boat and head for open water. For them, things and activities bring the most happiness. There's a lot of overlap with activities and people, I've noticed. If they love their road bike, they probably love their cycling club, too. It's other people *and* things that bring them joy.

But a few folks have also told me that they find happiness within. Their favorite time of the week might be yoga day, not only for the exercise but also for the perceived spiritual benefit of clearing their minds and finding peace inside themselves. They look forward to separating from people and things to focus on themselves. There, at that moment of meditation, they find happiness.

Never has the answer to my prompting been God. In fact, I can only count a handful of instances when people responded that faith is the fountain of their joy, but those were believers. And even then it's a rarity. Only after the conversation goes on a bit do believers amend their answers. "Well, of course it's God," they say after listing a few other things.

For apatheists, there is an incredible irony behind the answers I hear: they don't care about God, but they do care about joy. Yet apatheism thwarts one's pursuit of what humans desire most, lives of joy. We all want to be happy, to experience joy that inspires and lingers. Whether we find that joy in love or peace, in lifestyles or people, we spend all our free time and money searching for joy. The problem, though, is that joy is not something we find but rather something that finds us. Ironically, if we are indifferent to God, then we are indifferent to true joy, the very thing we desire most.

Phase One with Justin

I want to demonstrate how the first phase plays out through a fictional conversation with an apatheist named Justin, who is an amalgamation of three separate conversations I had with three real people. Two of them I knew personally, but the third was a stranger.

I met Justin at one of my favorite coffee shops. I don't recall how the conversation started, or even why, but it wasn't long until I was comfortable asking him about joy.

"So, Justin," I began, "tell me about what brings you the most joy in life."

"That's a good question," he said, pondering it for a moment.

Then he cracked a smile. "Definitely music, my band. I just get so much out of it, you know?"

Justin was a guitarist and vocalist. In fact, he was in town that weekend for a gig.

He went on to describe powerful experiences he'd had through writing lyrics and melodies. Crafting lyrics allowed him a safe avenue to process his escape from an abusive relationship. The band brought him in close contact with dear friends and opened his life up to other people whom he'd otherwise never have met. And music gave him a sense of meaning and purpose. Playing guitar made him feel valuable because he was creating something that other people might enjoy.

There was a pause in the conversation.

"Man, that's a good question," he reiterated.

I smiled and agreed.

"So, what about you?" he asked.

"For me, it has to be God, my faith."

"Oh," he responded. I could tell by his expression that he was expecting something a little more down to earth.

"So, you're into religion?" he asked.

"Yeah, for sure," I answered, and went on to explain how God is a source of joy because of who he is and what he has done.

He listened politely and even interjected some clarifying questions. But I could tell he didn't feel the same.

"If you don't mind me asking, do you have some kind of faith? I'm always curious what people think about God," I said.

"Eh," he replied. "No, not really."

He thought about his response a bit more. "I mean, I would say that I'm a Christian, but only because my parents are Catholic. I think it's important to be in sync with the spiritual side of your life. But I struggle to believe that something like God could exist, so it's not really something I think about all that often."

Things can easily veer off track at such a point in the conversation. How can Justin claim to be a Christian and find spirituality important but not believe in God? His response is an example of combinativeness. Justin combined ideas from Christianity and skepticism to form a customized belief system. The knee-jerk reaction to hearing Justin's beliefs is to object that he isn't truly a Christian or to correct him by classifying him as an agnostic. Doing so is a mistake. Letting Justin tell you who he is, after all, is the only way to get to know him. Early in the conversation, it's important to learn who Justin believes he is. It's true—Justin is not a Christian; he's agnostic. But he believes that some part of him warrants the Christian title.

"So," I asked, "you don't practice any kind of faith?"

He smiled and said, "My church is the stage."

I felt like he was trying to veer the conversation away from God back to music, so I drew us back in.

"And God, whether he exists or not, that's just . . ."

He interrupted, "It's just not that important to me, I guess. I'm glad that religion can make people happy, like you. You seem like a nice guy. And sometimes religion can be used to oppress people, like women and the gay community, or, you know, it can be misused. But, for me, it's just not a big deal."

"It?" I asked for clarification.

"God," he said. "I mean, that belief seems good for you, and that's great. So long as you don't force your belief on anyone else. But it's just not . . ." He hesitated. "It's not meant for everyone, I guess."

At this point, there was a bit of tension in the conversation. And it's easy to let go, to find something else to talk about to alleviate the mounting pressure. But this is the crucial point in the conversation, so I pressed in.

"I think belief in God is good for everyone," I said.

"Even if people don't want to believe?" he asked.

"Yeah, even so," I replied.

"Why do you think that?"

I'll share my answer to his question, but not just yet. Now is the time to talk about pivoting the conversation into its second phase.

Phase 2: What Is the Power and Permanence of Our Joy?

By this point, I know what my conversation partner finds to be the most essential thing in life. In essence, I know what kind of idols he worships, the created things from which he seeks meaning and joy. Now it's time for an uncomfortable question. What if the idol were destroyed? What if that source (or those sources) of happiness failed or disappeared? What would happen should the person lose his job or break up with her partner? I want each person with whom I engage in this manner to think about the *power* and *permanence* of his or her joy. How *powerful* is that hobby or friendship in terms of bringing joy in all seasons of life? How *permanent* is the joy received from communities or careers, no matter what happens? This is the part of the conversation where doubt comes in; it's the point of tension that must be pushed before I can communicate the desirability of Christianity.

Consider, for example, the power of money to bring joy. We're told, time and again, that money can't buy happiness. The saying is beyond cliché. But people still love mammon. We all know someone who claims that money doesn't bring them joy but acts as if it does. Their hands and families are calloused by corporate ladder climbing. There's a drive within them to accumulate as much as they can as fast as possible. The more they earn, the more they want to gain. For a growing number of people, it's not money but experiences they seek endlessly. For them, it's less about accumulating wealth than about authentic experiences that can enhance their uniqueness. But Augustine was right when he said that we cannot find the happy life until we can say of our joy, "This is sufficient; the happy life is here."[2] How much money or how many adventures do they need to say, "It is enough; it is there; my joy is complete in this wealth"? So I ask of those who find joy in wealth, "Is your source of joy powerful enough to tell you when you have enough?"

Similarly, not everything, nor everyone, we love can withstand the trials of life. When things get tough, we learn how fickle some friends can be. Just ask Job. "Joy" is quickly extinguished by betrayal and abandonment. Accidents or diseases restrict us from our favorite activities. What happens to the happily married marathoner when her husband leaves and she injures her leg in an accident? If her greatest joys were found in marriage and marathoning, what happens when both disappear?

These are uncomfortable questions, and sometimes they're morbid and upsetting to ask, but they must be asked. Testing our sources of joy opens us to the possibility that we aren't as secure in our happiness as we once thought. And if joy is something that everyone yearns for, because it is a crucial element to the fullness we all seek, then it's frightening to think that joy is fleeting.

In essence, these questions penetrate the buffered self. They get an apatheist past those protective barriers meant to block out any idea or experience he or she doesn't like. If I began the conversation by telling them they should believe in God because he could bring them joy, he or she would have shut down immediately. "It's great that God brings you joy," one of them might say, "but he's just not for me." Instead, they need to realize first that their joy, although real, is nevertheless incomplete and brittle. When we ask questions about joy first, we expose the frailty of their hope for happiness.

They begin to doubt, if even for a moment, whether or not the object of their joy can deliver what they hope for. This is a beneficial doubt, the kind that makes a person reassess what he or she believes and why he or she believes it. It's the doubt Kierkegaard spoke about, the kind that is better

---

[2] Augustine, *Confessions*, trans. Thomas Williams, 179 (see chap. 4, n. 9).

than objective thinking because it overrides apathy with interest. And planting this doubt is *key* to having a conversation about God with apatheists. They need to be interested in God to be able to consider him as a source of joy.

So far in the conversation between me and Justin I've recounted, we've not talked about much beyond him and his joy. God has barely made an appearance. He only came up in relation to *my* beliefs and fullness, not Justin's. This is when I share with an apatheist the source of ultimate joy for *all people*, especially God's power and permanence. Most importantly, I try to communicate that faith is not something I add to my life. Faith is an entirely new mode of existing. Christianity is not an accessory that we don or discard when desired. Faith and hope in Christ are the recreation and renewal of the whole person, both now and forever. We experience resurrection from death into life as a "new creation" in Christ (2 Cor 5:17). In him, we find powerful and permanent joy because his goodness and faithfulness touch every area of our lives. Regardless of whether or not things are going well at work and in relationships, we Christians still experience joy.

In short, I share the gospel. I don't expect them to understand what I'm saying, but—and this is key—they are ready to *listen*. Why? Because I don't start the conversations asking God questions they don't care about. Instead, we begin by discussing what makes them happy, and everyone is interested in talking about that. Had I started the conversation by asking them if they believed in God, we'd never have gotten so far. But because I started with *them* and *their* joy, the conversations have enough momentum to sustain them when I bring up God's joy for us.

Answering Objections in Gentleness

This is the point in the conversation when objections appear. The contestability and diversity of belief caused by secularism rush to the foreground. Sometimes I get questions like, "What makes you so sure that God exists?" or "How do you know *your* God exists?" But these are very rare. Objections usually involve the Bible and ethics. "Hasn't science disproved the Bible?" "Doesn't the Bible condone genocide and slavery?" "Isn't Christianity patriarchal and homophobic?"

There are no short answers to any of these objections, and my intention in bringing them up now is not to address them, as that is not the aim of this book. But, in my experience, objections will come. They are the scaffolding that supports the buffered self. They help apatheists maintain their lack of reason and motivation to care about God. So we need to address each objection as it comes.

It's daunting to hear such questions, to be sure, but it's also a good sign. These objections only come up because the apatheist is interested in talking about faith. It's vital that we honor their interest by dialoguing. How, exactly, that takes place is up to you. There is a wealth of resources to help on this front (see appendix). But I'd like to offer some advice in answering objections well.

First, I find it very important to stick to the topic at hand. G. K. Chesterton quipped, "All roads lead to Rome; which is one reason why many people never get there."[3] It's easy for the conversation to jump tracks from one objection to another. Don't let this happen. If the discussion is about biblical ethics and sexual orientation, I stay there. If the conversation is about the book of Genesis and science, I stick with it. I keep the conversation on one road and ride it all the way to Rome. Otherwise, I risk floating from one objection to another until we're both exhausted and frustrated, stranded in a field miles from the city on seven hills.

Speaking of frustration, I also find it very important to keep the temperature of the conversation cool. Evangelism perishes when the temperature of debate is hot enough to melt gentleness and respect. In the quintessential verse on apologetics, Peter commands us, "In your hearts regard Christ the Lord as holy, ready at any time to give a defense to anyone who asks you for a reason for the hope that is in you" (1 Pet 3:15). What we are called to is "defense" (Greek, *apologia*), or "to give an answer" or "to explain" why we

---

[3] G. K. Chesterton, *Orthodoxy* (New York: Dodd, Mead, 1950), 153.

believe our faith. But *how* do we give our defense, our responses to objections? Peter continues, "Yet do this with gentleness and reverence" (1 Pet 3:16a). We give an answer for our faith in gentleness, which is challenging, especially when we're called closed-minded or intolerant. But we must follow Christ's example, to "be kind, always showing gentleness to all people" and letting our "graciousness be known to everyone" (Titus 3:2; Phil 4:5). Gentleness is part of the flavor we taste in the fruit of the Spirit (Gal 5:23). It's a good thing, a holy thing.

Finally, I have to remember why I'm having a spiritual conversation with an apatheist in the first place. It's not to win arguments. I want apatheists to long for God with right affection. I want to see their apathetic disbelief transform into a fervor for the gospel. I want them to love the Lord their God with all their hearts, souls, minds, and strength.

Phase Two with Justin

At this point in my coffee house conversation, I could tell Justin wasn't ready to talk about God directly. He obviously didn't care about him, and the gospel felt foreign and strange.

I said, "Can I ask a personal question?"

"Sure," Justin said, tentatively.

"You love music. It brings you joy. God forbid, there comes a day when the band breaks up or you can't play guitar for whatever reason. That's a realistic scenario, right?"

He agreed.

"I mean, it's a sad thought, for sure," I continued. "I love my family. I love activities like kayaking and hiking. But life is filled with tragedy, and those things are often taken away from us."

I let the thought hang for a moment.

"Say the day comes when music is taken from you. What is the greatest source of joy in your life then?"

The entire conversation hinges on this or a similar challenging and uncomfortable question. It's a question that introduces an unwelcomed (but necessary) doubt into the apatheist's mind. I've found that most people aren't willing to move beyond it. The better you know someone, the more likely they are to stay with you. Justin, though, was one of those rare strangers who felt like a friend.

"Man, you're filled with good questions," he said with a laugh, alleviating the tension. "Um," he searched for the answer, "I guess family."

"Oh, you're married?" I asked, misunderstanding what he meant.

"No, I have a girlfriend, but it's a serious relationship. And I'm thinking more like all family," he clarified.

"And, God forbid, what happens if you two break up or your family becomes fractured by stress or death or whatever?"

Again, here is the goal of these questions: to remove the roof off the apatheist's life. Looking in, we discovered the beam that supported his joy was found to be weaker than he thought. An inconsistency revealed itself. Justin lived as if he had lasting joy, but, in reality, he was only experiencing fragile happiness. His beliefs were shown to be more brittle than he thought. For the first time, he doubted something that he'd taken for granted just moments ago. And that's an upsetting experience.

Even though emotions had been stirred, Justin was ready to talk about God. His interest was captured.

"I get where you're going with this," he barked.

The answer was obvious, but he wouldn't say it. Instead, he turned the tables on me.

"What about you? What happens if you lose everything?" he asked.

I replied, "My joy doesn't come primarily from things that I can lose. It comes from something that can't be lost."

"Right, I get it," he said, a bit flustered. "God is immortal or whatever. I'm asking what happens when the things that bring you joy are taken away?"

"That's one of the beautiful things about my faith. Christianity is a faith through which one finds joy *because of* God, who sustains joy *in spite of* grief and sorrow and loss."

At this point in such conversations, I revisit the gospel to double-click on the paradox of Christian belief—that ultimate joy is found in the death of Christ. The saving activity of God elicited joy in Christ *in spite of* the libel, slander, injustice, abuse, and death he experienced. The resurrection proved it.

"So the joy I experience in faith is both *because of* God's activity and *in spite of* the suffering we face in life," I concluded.

Justin clearly wanted to push hard against this point, so he mustered the courage to ask a difficult question:

"Even if you lost your wife—and, man, I'm not saying that's something I'd wish on my worst enemy—but you're telling me that you'd still be happy?"

"Oh, no, not at all. The opposite of happy," I clarified. "I'd be wrecked. Anger, sorrow, grief, depression, all of it. But, nevertheless, I'd still have joy."

"What's the difference?" he asked.

I explained how finding ultimate happiness in created things is temporary, fleeting, and fickle. Then I spoke about why finding ultimate joy in God is long-lasting, enduring, and static.

"And it's because of God that I have that joy," I concluded.

Justin let the thought simmer for a moment. He hadn't really considered the difference between earthly happiness and heavenly joy.

"All right," Justin said, conjuring up his objection. "What if you lose your faith? Where would your joy come from then?"

"What do you mean?" I asked.

"What happens if you stop believing in God?"

This is a great question, one that comes up often. But notice that Justin is talking about God. This wouldn't have happened had I started the conversation by asking, "What do you believe about God?" He would have simply sloughed it off. Now, though, belief in God is central to a topic that he is interested in.

I replied: "I suppose, then, that my joy would evaporate with my disbelief."

Justin seemed caught off guard by my response. Perhaps he expected me to double down, saying that nothing could prevent me from believing. But that's not where I prefer to go, nor is it even honest.

"You see," I continued, "God's existence isn't contingent on my belief in him. In other words, God exists regardless of whether or not anyone believes in him."

Justin thought for a moment. I could see he had an objection ready but hesitated to ask.

"Okay, you seem like a reasonable guy," he finally said, complimenting me before objecting. "How can you believe in God with all the science out there proving that he doesn't exist?"

I rehearsed the litany of arguments for God's existence. We went back and forth, but I kept the temperature of the conversation cool. *Jesus is Lord over this conversation*, I reminded myself, *so treat Justin with the kind of gentleness that flows from the Holy Spirit.*

Phase 3: How Does Joy Find Us?

At this point in the conversation, it's time to land the plane. I know the time has come when the conversation gets trapped in a cul-de-sac. The objections and arguments have taken the conversation as far as it can go. And, honestly, there's little chance that apologetics will completely change a person's mind. Skeptics dig deeper into their skepticism; believers hunker down in their faith. But with exposure to different beliefs comes an inevitable shift. Perhaps the apatheist hasn't considered that Christianity might have good reasons for its beliefs. Maybe now he or she will realize Christians don't leap blindly into the darkness of faith after all.

The goal is not to change apatheists' minds right there on the spot. Instead, we aim to challenge their beliefs and reorient their hearts. In essence, exposure to apologetics swats away distractions so that we can get back to what matters most—the gospel, the great story of how Joy finds us.

I've discovered that if apatheists are still with me by this point, then they are willing to listen to the gospel. They're invested. I feel like I know them; more importantly, they feel known by me. Even though I've made them uncomfortable, doubting their joy has made them curious about mine. And because God is my joy, they are now interested in him. This is when I tell them the story of the gospel, and I do mean *story*. I don't explain the gospel as a set of religious propositions. I tell the gospel as the story of good news in a language they'll understand with the Bible as my basis.

Why? Because there is power in storytelling, which is why the gospel itself is a story of redemption.

The Power of Gospel Storytelling

We love stories. We listen to them all the time. During our morning commutes, we stream the latest episode of *This American Life.* In the office, we gather around the water coolers to hear tales of weekend adventures from our colleagues. In the evenings, we rehearse the day's events when our spouses ask, "How was your day?" At dusk, we read the Bible and children's books to our kids before bed. At night, we continue to create and act in the stories of our dreams. We're obsessed with stories. Some scientists believe that we're actually wired for them.[4] A good story with tension and meaning holds our attention long enough to actually change the way we think and feel. No wonder the Bible is one grand story about God's redemptive work through his Son from creation to new creation.

Stories compel us because they draw on the power of imagination to penetrate our hearts and minds. They have an uncanny ability to sneak past our barricades of belief, invade our buffered selves, and change us without our permission and sometimes even our awareness.

The hearts and minds of apatheists are hidden behind a buffer of apathy. They want to maintain their lack of reason and motivation to care about God. We can't beat down that buffer with religious facts and arguments, but we can sneak past it with stories. The best way I've found—the way that the Holy Spirit relishes to bless my labor—is through gospel storytelling.

The way I frame the gospel story is in terms of Joy finding us. God is a pursuer, an initiator. He comes to us even when we're uninterested or

---

[4] See Steven Pinker, *How the Mind Works* (New York: W. W. Norton, 2009), 538–43; Brian Boyd, *On the Origin of Stories: Evolution, Cognition, and Fiction* (Cambridge, MA: Harvard University Press, 2009), 129–208; Paul Armstrong, *How Literature Plays with the Brain: The Neuroscience of Reading and Art* (Baltimore: Johns Hopkins University Press, 2013).

running away from him. We sin against him. We rebel, but, all the same, he persists. It's part of his good and faithful nature to find us.

Finding us was the first thing God did after we fell. A long time ago, the Bible says, two people lived with God in a garden. Everything was "very good"—no sadness, no betrayal, no anxiety, no depression, no lies, no disobedience, and, best of all, no death. But the book of Genesis tells us that this only lasted for so long. Our ancestors, Adam and Eve, rebelled against God and fell from grace after listening to and believing his enemy. With that fall came death, the ultimate sorrow (Genesis 3). It wasn't kept just to them—death spread to everyone who came after Adam and Eve (Rom 5:12–14).

They tried to hide their sin, but God is omniscient, all-knowing. He knew what happened. We might imagine God demanding Adam and Eve pull themselves together and seek him. But that's not what happened. God sought them. When he found them, he promised them that one day he would make things right. Even though they bore punishment for sinning, and even though they grieved and were in sorrow, God promised that one day mankind would live in joy again (Gen 3:13–15).

Centuries later, God began to move on his promise to humanity. He chose one man, Abraham, to be the father of an entire nation. God promised Abraham that he would father a son. Abraham's grandson would father a nation that would one day have its own homeland. Abraham believed this promise, and by faith alone, God considered him righteous; Abraham was saved (Gen 15:6; 17:1–8; Rom 4:2–3).

Years later, it became evident that God was staying true to his promise. The Hebrew nation was born from Abraham, but there was one problem: they weren't living freely in their homeland. Just the opposite was true. The Hebrews were enslaved by a foreign nation, Egypt (Exod 1:1–14). But God wasn't going to leave his people in slavery forever. He came to them through Moses. God found the Hebrews in sorrow and grief, and he had had enough. God wanted his people to experience joy. So, through a man named Moses, he led them out of slavery and into their promised land. And he promised his people that so long as they remained faithful, he would always be with them (Exod 19:3–6).

But they didn't remain faithful. They couldn't. The sin they inherited from Adam was too powerful. It permeates our hearts and our minds, our desires and our thoughts. No matter how hard God's people tried, they failed over and again. God came to them and pursued them through a line of prophets. Each time God raised up a prophet, the people would often ignore and reject him. At best, they repented for a season. But it was just that—a temporary, fleeting season (1 Sam 8:7–9; Matt 23:34–35; Heb 1:1).

For a time, it seemed God had given up on his people. But he is good, faithful, and able. He pursues us because he loves us. So, just like he did in the garden, God came to us. This time he did so through his Son, Jesus Christ (John 1:1–3, 14; Gal 4:4). He walked among us. He experienced the human condition, living the way we live. He had a family, friends, a job. He laughed and cried, felt happiness and sorrow. He lived our life, yet without a single fault or flaw (2 Cor 5:21; Heb 4:15–16).

At the appropriate time, he pursued individuals, calling them to be his followers. Then he began to do miraculous things, miracles that pointed to his divine nature. He reminded God's people that they were meant for more than death and sorrow. They were meant for life and joy (John 3:16; 4:13–14; 10:10–11).

Not everyone liked this message. Greedy and selfish men among Abraham's descendants had built a system of religious power to control their people. But Jesus was a radical. He confronted their lies, and people started to believe him. The religious people conspired against him, and had him executed on a cross, despite his being an innocent man.

And even though it seems like the story would have to end there, it didn't. Three days after Jesus's death, he came back to life. And the first thing he did was find his followers. He approached his disciples, he convinced them that he was the same Jesus they remembered, and he encouraged them (1 Cor 15:3–8). They were filled with joy (Acts 13:52). And this joy motivated the early Christians to spread this good news.

They taught that every single human is broken. We are what the Bible calls "sinners" (Ps 51:5, cf. Rom 5:8). We sin and we are sinned against (Rom 3:23; 6:23). Each of us conspires to rebel against God's holiness in our hearts; we act on that evil in all kinds of ways, and we fall short of God's perfect standard (Ps 51:1–3). Brokenness and wrongness and injustice oppress us all our lives because of this (Ps 12:1–8). And we contribute to the bad experiences of others. We break things and people. We do wrong to ourselves, others, and God (Rom 3:9–18). We, too, are oppressors—every one of us. For this reason, the Bible teaches, we deserve grief, sorrow, and death forever (Rom 2:5–16).

But God, who is beyond any goodness we can comprehend, stayed true to the promises that he made to Adam, Abraham, and Abraham's descendants.

His incredible love for all humanity, in fact, makes us alive through faith in the message of Jesus. God saves us by grace, a love that we don't deserve (Eph 2:8–9). We receive salvation not through cleaning ourselves up, but by letting God's Spirit cover us with the faithfulness of Jesus. Through faith in him alone, we are lifted up with him (Rom 8:1–2). The cross and empty tomb have upended the world. We live in a new reality, one in which Christ reigns over all things. We live in a new kingdom, one in which sin has no claim over us. Happiness and trials come and go, but our joy will always remain. And when we die, we don't stay dead. We rise up from death and are carried through judgement to sit with Christ in his forever life and endless love (John 6:40; 14:1–4; Rom 8:30; 2 Cor 5:1–8). Joy finds us and will keep us for eternity.

Your Role as a Living Example of the Gospel

Now, for most of us, telling the gospel story ends there. But it shouldn't. If you've placed your faith in Christ, aren't you a part of God's story of redemption?

Remember, when it's all said and done, you are the best apologetic. You display the power of the gospel. Show how your inclusion in God's story, your *joy because of* God's redemption, has given you joy through all seasons of life, your *joy in spite of* sorrow and trials.

In other words, share your testimony. Tell them how God pursued you and is pursuing him or her, even in that moment. Right then, right there, right now. The joy they are looking for in themselves, others, and things is neither powerful nor permanent enough to rest their hearts. Invite them to give faith a chance, to take a risk and search the Scriptures.

After that, leave the apatheist in the hands of the Holy Spirit. Rest easy knowing that you are not their savior, but that their Savior has spoken to them through you.

To the on-mission man discussed in Matt 25:14-30, the Master said, "Well done, good and faithful servant." Those are the words we should long to hear from our Lord Jesus.

Placing Pebbles in Shoes

But what if, after all that, they remain apathetic? What if he ignores it all and sticks to his lack of reason and motivation not to care? It's a disheartening thing to watch a person just walk away from the conversation. And, more often than not, they do. But just know, the person you invest in is walking away *with* something that wasn't there before. Something that will pester him.

I love hiking. Next to kayaking, it's my favorite activity in the world. I love wandering in the forest, overwhelmed by fresh air, watching the branches sway to the soundtrack of bird songs. Hiking is liberating. The wilderness is unknown and unsafe, yet familiar and relaxing. And I like the exercise it provides. I find myself getting into a comfortable pace, stopping only to rest or take in a view.

But there is one thing I can't stand about hiking—pebbles. You know those annoying little rocks that hitch a ride in your shoe? They like to wedge themselves in between the ball of your foot and the sole of your boot like a stowaway hitching a ride on a ship in search of a better life. There, they rub and irritate and burrow into your skin with every step. I get these pebbles in my shoes every so often, and each time I do, I lie to myself that I will walk it off. The longer I hike, the theory goes, the more likely the pebble will shift to a tolerable space in my boot until I decide to stop and rest. But that never works. Inevitably, the little stone becomes so unbearable that it decides for me when I stop to rest. I plop on the ground, remove my hiking boot, and jostle it around until the little annoyance is cast out. Few things annoy me more on the trail than pebbles in my shoes.

Imagine life as a hike on a trail. What causes us to stop? Rest, of course, is probably the main reason. We get tired, so we need to stop for a moment. We take a vacation, enjoy a long weekend, or just zone out by binge-watching our favorite series. We also stop to take in the scenery. The beauty that life offers captures our attention, and we can't look away. The newness of a romantic relationship or the arrival of a newborn child pauses our lives at work and with friends. Nothing else in the world seems to matter in those moments. We stop hiking, just for a short time, to take in the scenery of love and life.

But there's another reason we stop—pebbles. These pebbles are doubts, hesitations, and uncertainties. We try to live with those vexing things as long as we can, but in the long run, there comes the point when we can't take another step. It's too annoying, too painful. So we stop and take the time to examine what's bothering us. One of the goals of evangelism is to place gospel pebbles in shoes, to plant truths that will dig into the souls of our neighbors. Sure, a person may walk away from a gospel conversation seemingly unfazed, but that will only last for a mile or so down the trail. Eventually, he or she will have to stop and untie their beliefs, peering into them to see why that truth is bothering them so much.

The pebble in my conversation boils down to my questions about the listener's source of joy. I want him or her to ask soul-piercing questions like, "What is my greatest source of joy?" "Is my joy powerful enough to sustain me through life's darkest seasons?" "Is my joy permanent enough to remain through life's most challenging difficulties?" If the conversation ended at that point, I'd consider it a success. Perhaps, for the first time, the apatheist will recognize that the happiness found in creation is temporary and fleeting. Sure, it's filling now, but it can be taken away, and usually is. The thought that there might be joy beyond our experience is haunting, and God can work through it.

But it's even better if I get to tell them about my joy because it is found in the gospel. Sure, a person might not understand all I said, but that's okay.

Neither did Nicodemus understand what Jesus meant by the necessity of being born again (John 3:1–15). A long time later, however, after Jesus's crucifixion, it's apparent that Nicodemus had come to trust in Jesus to the point that he tended his corpse (John 19:38–41).

Once a pebble is placed, doubt will irritate an apatheist until he or she can no longer stand the uncertainty. His or her image of fullness has been challenged. That's when the frailty and impermanence of their joy lifts their heads heavenward, causing them to look beyond the happiness that creation offers.

The Holy Spirit is on the move, tilling apathy to plant seeds of joy.

Phase Three with Justin

At this point at the coffee house, the arguments were exhausted. We'd reached the end of the conversational cul-de-sac with nowhere else to go. So I took us back to where we started—joy. This time, however, I intentionally changed the question.

"Can I tell you how joy found me?" I asked.

"H-how it *found* you?" Justin asked for clarification.

"Yeah, how it found me," I replied.

I unfolded the story of God's redemptive work in the world. How humanity fell from grace, why sin merits death, and the fact that every person—no matter who they are or what they believe—has fallen short of God's glory. But the good news is that God didn't leave us in sin. He sent his Son to rescue us through living a sinless life and dying an atoning death. Then, three days later, he came to life again, defeating sin and death forever for those who trust in him. Now, through faith in the person and work of Jesus, we, too, can experience a new life now and forever. And no matter what may come, we can rejoice always.

I also wove my story into God's story, explaining how I found joy in God because he found me. Before I was a believer, I looked for happiness in all the wrong places—in other people, in things, and within myself. I had idols, lots of them. My pursuit of happiness led me away from God and left me empty. But, despite my rebellion, God pursued me anyway, following me at every turn. That is, until one day when he decided to pounce. At a low moment of sorrow, I reached for a Bible gifted to me by my Christian grandmother. I opened it randomly to the middle, to Psalm 51 (KJV), and began to read: "Have mercy upon me, O God, according to thy lovingkindness. . . . Against thee, thee only, have I sinned. . . . Create in me a clean heart, O God; and renew a right spirit within me. . . . Restore unto me the joy of thy salvation." I didn't quite understand what that meant, but I knew that I wanted what this prayer sought. In that moment, I realized that my search for happiness was a fool's errand, and that only through repentance and forgiveness could I find joy. I repented in prayer to God, and he renewed my soul. Joy found me.

"Joy is at the heart of the Christian faith," I concluded. "And, for me, faith isn't just something I do. It's not like an ornament I add to my life because it works for me. It fundamentally changes my whole mode of living. So, because joy is at the center of my faith, every aspect of my life is touched by it."

Very little of what I said made sense to Justin just then, but that's okay. "Faith comes from what is heard, and what is heard comes through the message about Christ" (Rom 10:17). The Spirit uses every single instance the gospel is spoken for his purpose and glory, regardless of whether it bears an immediate or obvious harvest.

As the conversation ends and you part ways, remember that your role in your listener's life isn't over. Pray for them. Pray that the Holy Spirit would bless your encounter, that the gospel would take root in spite of their apathy, and that God's will will be done on earth.

Chapter 8 | Go, Therefore, to the Apathetic

As providence would have it, I bumped into the Muslim man in Cambridge about six months after our first encounter. I only knew it was him because, once again, he was standing behind a booth proselytizing. This time, he had company. There were a few other Muslims accompanying him, attempting to hand out tracts and copies of the Qur'an.

As I approached the booth, the man noticed me and smiled. "Ah, friend, it's been a long time!" he said, remembering me as I had recognized him. Apparently, the coffee and conversation made a lasting impression.

"Yes, it has," I said, greeting him with a handshake.

"What, no coffee for me this time?" he asked with a smile.

We made small talk, catching up on life and recent events. I wanted to know if he remembered our talk, specifically what he said about apatheism.

I said, "I'm not sure if you'll remember, but you said something that really stuck with me the last time we spoke."

"No, what's that?" he inquired.

"About how people don't care about God."

"Ah, yes," he replied, "and not much has changed in my experience." He gestured to boxes full of religious reading material tucked beneath the table. "I can't even give this stuff away."

I asked him how he coped with rejection due to apathy, and about his role as a representative of his religion in the face of apatheism.

"Well," he started, "if I'm honest, it's not really my place to worry about whether or not they care."

He then described himself as less an ambassador and more like a warning sign, merely an announcement of judgment to come. He felt that he had done everything in his power to put God on display. If, after all that, the people he encountered still didn't care to believe, then it wasn't any of his concern. His attitude had shifted considerably from the dejection I'd seen earlier that year.

"So," he concluded, "whether or not they care isn't my problem. I'm simply a messenger."

Of course, not all Muslims share his perspective. I don't want to paint everyone with the same stroke. But this one man's chilly distance from the people he once cared about caused me to reflect on my own approach to apatheism. Is it the Christian's responsibility to merely relay information from a joyful heaven to an apathetic earth? Or are we called to a tougher challenge, one that, by the power of the Holy Spirit, plants a taste of heaven's joy deep within the heart of the apatheist?

At the beginning of the book, I asked whether we are living in an Athens without a statue to the unknown god, one in which citizens no longer care much about the gods, robbing us of the minimally common interest in theism that we've enjoyed for the better part of two millennia in Western society. To answer my own question, yes, of course, I believe that we are. Our figurative Athenians are leaving the Areopagus, and, for those of us who remain, there are only two options.

We could despair and surrender to indifference, deciding it's just too hard to share the gospel with people who aren't interested. If people don't want to listen, why should we bother them? We could wash our hands of it all, throwing them up in the air while letting out exasperated sighs. Like the Muslim man, we could simply abandon the house of apatheism to its fate and dust off our feet as we surround ourselves with only other believers.

If so, we'll drift into our own kind of apathy. Our hearts will grow distant from our neighbors as our concern for them fades. We will let bygones be bygones. If they don't want to care, how can we make them? There isn't a Cupid's arrow for affection toward God, so we ought to let them be.

But there's a second option. One that looks at apatheism not as an insurmountable challenge but as a unique opportunity for evangelism, the likes of which the world has never seen. We can pioneer a new frontier of evangelism with the Spirit's help. Rarely, if ever, in the history of our faith have Christians faced the kind of indifference toward God that we experience today. So we ought to explore and employ ways to seed the gospel in this wilderness of apathy. After all, the kingdom of Christ knows no boundary nor borders (Luke 1:33).

This is the option that the Great Commission demands: to go and make disciples of all nations, and, by extension, those of all attitudes toward God. It's tough work, to be sure. But tilling and planting aren't meant to be easy. By the sweat of our brows we eat bread, and by spiritual sweat, we plant the message of the Bread of Life.

By "tough work," I don't mean to say that we ought to coerce people into loving God. Neither should we even try. It's odd to imagine someone arguing their neighbor into a loving relationship with their Creator. Instead, the tough work starts in our own hearts. We must first examine ourselves to ensure that we are joyful witnesses. We have to ask ourselves the hard questions: Have I been affected by our apathetic age? Does my life model the happiness and joy I claim to experience? Can I guide apatheists to the joy of Christ by example, not just instruction; by deeds, not just words?

Only after the Spirit has worked on our own hearts can we be used to invite other hearts into the kingdom. Even then, the tough work has only begun. We must toil with grace, which requires patience, humility, and trust. Grace allows space for apathy to thaw. Grace admits that apathy isn't "their" problem but a universal issue. Grace is big enough to work even when it feels like we've failed. For reasons like these, the apostle Paul said, "Let your speech always be gracious, seasoned with salt, so that you may know how you should answer each person" (Col 4:6). *Each* person, even the apathetic one.

In short, we must be joyful witnesses in our apathetic age, no matter the cost. When we are, the Lord Jesus promises his presence will be with us. "And remember," he taught the first disciples, "I am with you always, to the end of the age" (Matt 28:20).

Above all, sharing the gospel with apatheists will require a lot of prayer. There will be times when it feels like conversations are going nowhere, if they even start. We'll not be able to find the right words to challenge and invite apatheists to feel something for God. Trying will seem like failure and we'll be tempted to give up. But prayer is miraculously powerful. Prayer is how God carries us further than we ever imagine. The Holy Spirit intervenes, helping us in our weakness when we don't know what to say (Rom 8:26). He knows our hearts and minds, our worries and fears, our hopes and dreams. He testifies of Christ in ways we can't explain (John 15:26), and his sacrificial love draws all people to him (John 12:32). It's amazing how the Spirit works when we think there is no hope.

I experienced something like this recently with someone. We were talking about joy, but the conversation wasn't going the way I had envisioned or hoped. I'm sad to admit that I became frustrated with the conversation and gave up. But before I walked away, I was burdened to pray with him. I asked if he'd like prayer and, to my surprise, he was genuinely glad I asked.

During the prayer, I said something along the lines that the most precious thing a disciple of Christ can hope to hear is, "Well done, good and faithful servant." I ended the prayer shortly after quoting the parable (Matt 25:21–23; Luke 19:17). When I opened my eyes, I noticed that he was staring at the floor. I thought to myself that he hadn't listened at all. His mind had obviously been elsewhere the entire prayer, or so I assumed. But that's when it happened. He looked at me with deep sincerity and said, "I'm terrified that I won't hear that." His confession confused me, so I asked what he meant. "The part about being a faithful servant. I can't do it; I know that I'm not a good steward of my life."

I was beside myself. Here was a guy who, just a few minutes earlier, told me that he cared nothing for faith and God. Our conversation had gone nowhere. And, yet, something had since pressed his heart to the point that it was as if he'd become a different person in a matter of seconds. We spent the next hour talking about the gospel. What other power can so radically change a person's orientation toward God than God himself?

It is in the providential hands of God that we ought to rest our efforts by prayer. After it's all said and done, after we've shared the joy of truth and love in grace, we leave the results of each encounter to the Lord. He alone is the One who ignites true love and right passion.

APPENDIX: SUGGESTED READINGS ON APOLOGETICS

Craig, William Lane. *Reasonable Faith: Christian Truth and Apologetics*. 3rd ed. Wheaton, IL: Crossway Books, 2008.

Fesko, John V. *Reforming Apologetics: Retrieving the Classic Reformed Approach to Defending the Faith*. Grand Rapids: Baker Academic, 2019.

Frame, John. *Christianity Considered: A Guide for Skeptics and Seekers.* Bellingham, WA: Lexham Press, 2018.

Gould, Paul M. *Cultural Apologetics: Renewing the Christian Voice, Conscience, and Imagination in a Disenchanted World*. Grand Rapids: Zondervan, 2019.

Keller, Timothy. *The Reason for God: Belief in an Age of Skepticism*. New York: Penguin Books, 2016.

Lennox, John C. *Can Science Explain Everything?* Epsom, UK: Good Book Company, 2019.

Lewis, Clive S. *Mere Christianity*. New York: HarperCollins, 2017.

McLaughlin, Rebecca. *Confronting Christianity: 12 Hard Questions for the World's Largest Religion*. Wheaton, IL: Crossway, 2019.

Pearcey, Nancy. *Total Truth: Liberating Christianity from Its Cultural Captivity*. Wheaton, IL: Crossway, 2004.

————. *Finding Truth: 5 Principles for Unmasking Atheism, Secularism, and Other God Substitutes.* Colorado Springs, CO: David C. Cook, 2015.

Plantinga, Alvin. *Knowledge and Christian Belief.* Grand Rapids: Eerdmans, 2015.

Schaeffer, Francis. *The Francis A. Schaeffer Trilogy: Three Essential Books in One Volume.* Wheaton, IL: Crossway, 1990.

Sire, James W. *The Universe Next Door: A Basic Worldview Catalog.* 5th ed. Downers Grove, IL: InterVarsity Press, 2009.

————. *Apologetics beyond Reason: Why Seeing Really Is Believing.* Downers Grove, IL: InterVarsity Press, 2014.

White, James Emory. *Christianity for People Who Aren't Christians* (Grand Rapids: Baker Books, 2019).

Williams, Peter J. *Can We Trust the Bible?* Wheaton, IL: Crossway, 2018.

SUBJECT INDEX

SCRIPTURE INDEX